Easy Lotus® 1-2-3®

Shelley O'Hara

Easy Lotus® 1-2-3®

Library of Congress Catalog No.: 91-62459

ISBN: 0-88022-799-0

93 92 91 6 5 4 3 2 1

Interpretation of the printing code: the rightmost double-digit number is the year of the book's printing; the rightmost single-digit number, the number of the book's printing. For example, a printing code of 91-1 shows that the first printing of the book occurred in 1991.

Screen reproductions in this book were created using Collage Plus from Inner Media, Inc., Hollis, NH.

Easy Lotus 1-2-3 is based on Lotus 1-2-3 Version 2.3.

Publisher: Lloyd J. Short

Associate Publisher: Karen A. Bluestein

Project Development Manager: Mary Bednarek

Managing Editor: Paul Boger

Book Design: Scott Cook, Karen A. Bluestein

Illustrations: Scott Cook

Production Team: Hilary Adams, Sandy Grieshop, Michele Laseau, Bruce Steed

Series Director
Karen A. Bluestein

Project Leader
Kathie-Jo Arnoff

Production Editor
Cindy Morrow

Editor
Patricia A. Brooks

Technical Editor
Robin Drake

Novice Reviewers
Janis Fechalos

Contents at a Glance

Contents

Introduction

Introduction

1-2-3 is a spreadsheet program, which is an electronic accountant's pad. Rather than total figures using a pencil and column-ruled paper, you enter data into a 1-2-3 worksheet. You then can manipulate the data in that worksheet. With a spreadsheet program, you can perform simple mathematical operations such as addition, subtraction, multiplication, and division. You can also calculate very complex, involved equations.

You can use 1-2-3 to keep track of facts (clients, for example) and figures (sales results, for example). You can create simple worksheets or complex financial models.

You can use 1-2-3 to create a variety of worksheets, including

Budget

	Qtr 1	Qtr 2	Qtr 3	Qtr 4
Rent	10,000	10,000	10,000	10,000
Utilities	1,600	1,500	1,800	1,600
Supplies	320	320	320	320
Salaries	30,000	30,000	30,000	30,000
Taxes	1,500	500	500	500
Other	3,000	2,000	2,500	3,500
Total	$46,420	$44,320	$45,120	$45,920

- Home Budget
- Business Budget
- Sales Report
- Business Expense Report
- Financial Report
- Check Register

- Inventory List
- Personnel List
- Client List
- Grade List

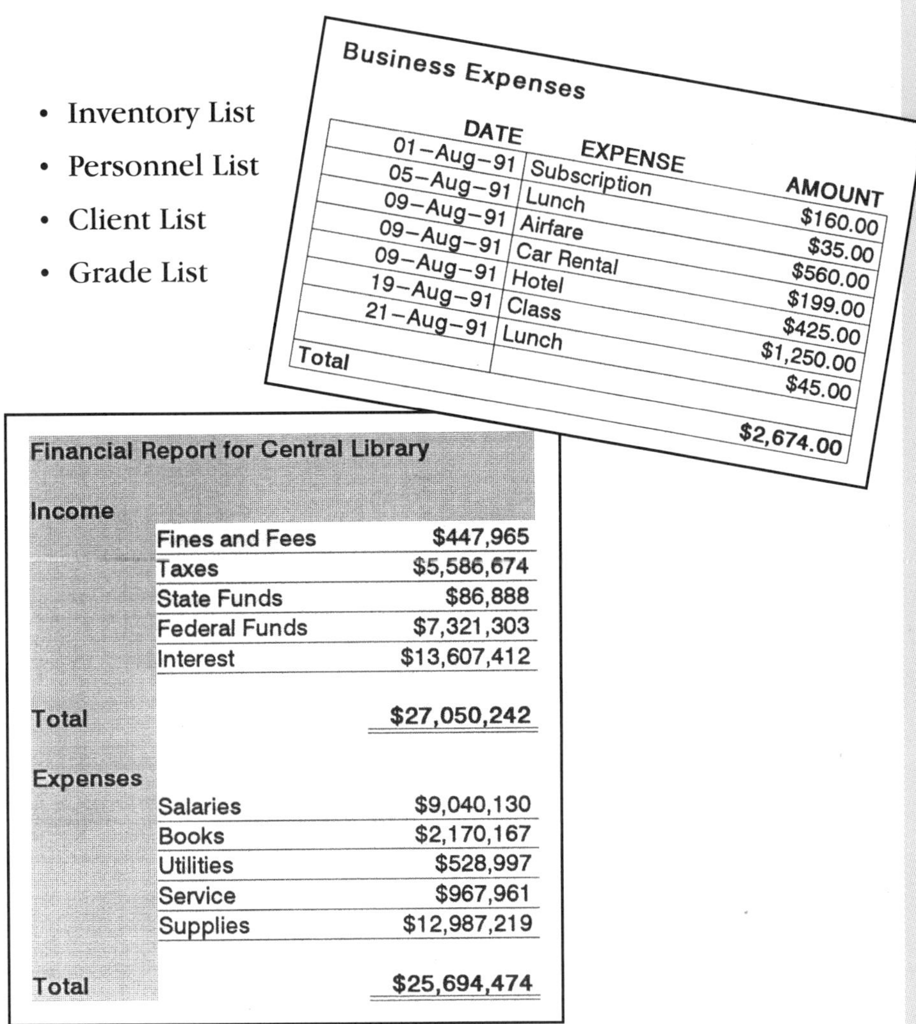

Business Expenses

DATE	EXPENSE	AMOUNT
01–Aug–91	Subscription	$160.00
05–Aug–91	Lunch	$35.00
09–Aug–91	Airfare	$560.00
09–Aug–91	Car Rental	$199.00
09–Aug–91	Hotel	$425.00
19–Aug–91	Class	$1,250.00
21–Aug–91	Lunch	$45.00
Total		$2,674.00

Financial Report for Central Library

Income		
	Fines and Fees	$447,965
	Taxes	$5,586,674
	State Funds	$86,888
	Federal Funds	$7,321,303
	Interest	$13,607,412
Total		**$27,050,242**
Expenses		
	Salaries	$9,040,130
	Books	$2,170,167
	Utilities	$528,997
	Service	$967,961
	Supplies	$12,987,219
Total		**$25,694,474**

You can use 1-2-3 to perform these functions:

Calculate. You can write simple formulas to add, subtract, multiply, and divide figures. You tell 1-2-3 what numbers to use, and you can depend on 1-2-3 to calculate the results correctly every time.

Change data and recalculate. When you change, add, or delete data, 1-2-3 recalculates results automatically. There's no erasing and rewriting when you forget a crucial figure.

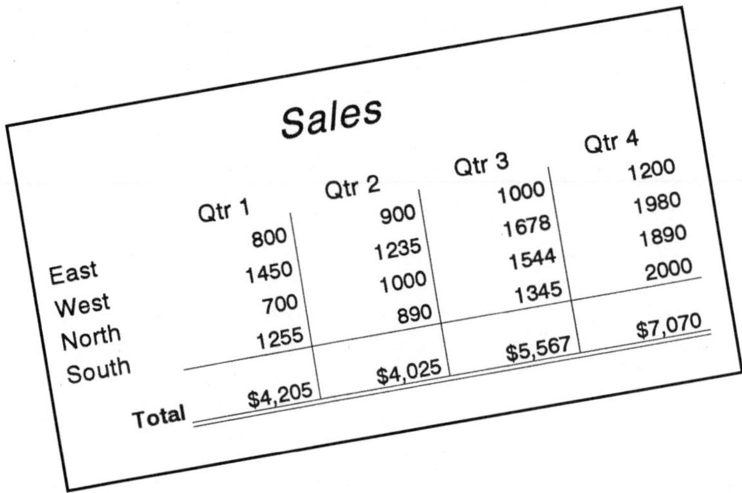

Rearrange data. With your worksheet on-screen, you can add or delete a column or row. You can copy and move data from one place to another.

Repeat information. You can copy text, a value, or a formula to another place in the worksheet. For example, suppose that you create a monthly budget worksheet that totals the expenses for each month. You could write a formula in 1-2-3 that calculates January's totals; then you could copy this formula for February through December.

Reverse changes. The Undo feature in 1-2-3 enables you to restore data that you just deleted, moved, or copied back to its original form.

Change the format of data. You can format your results many different ways. For example, you can display a number with dollar signs, as a percentage, or as a date. You can align text left, right, or center.

Add enhancements. The heart of 1-2-3 is its calculation capabilities, but the results are what you use. In addition to controlling how data is displayed, you can call attention to results by adding shading, underlining data, drawing a box around data, or adding headers and footers.

Copy and reuse your worksheet. You can make a copy of a worksheet and make changes to the copy to create a second, different worksheet. For example, you can use the same format for a sales worksheet for each division of your company. Use the copy, enter the new data, and you have a new worksheet.

You can create thousands of worksheets in 1-2-3. For example, you can use the program to keep track of stocks, investments, and inventory. You can create balance sheets and income statements. You can calculate personal or business expenses. You can keep lists of clients and employees.

These examples show just a couple of the worksheets that you can create using 1-2-3.

Real Estate Client List

Last Name	First Name	Phone	Price Range	Bedrooms
Francis	Zoe	555–0095	$88,000	3
James	Evan	555–7288	$140,000	4
Kubiack	Larry	555–4343	$175,000	5
McMichael	Sean	555–5666	$325,000	5
Oppen	Lois	555–6901	$59,000	2
Pantuso	Ernie	555–1215	$120,000	4
Price	Carolyn	555–7843	$250,000	5
Rich	Robin	555–4082	$69,000	2
Roth	Zachary	555–4322	$100,000	3

Why You Need This Book

1-2-3's numerous features make working with numbers easy. Using this program saves you time and makes your work more efficient. But learning to use the many features is difficult at first, which is why you need this book.

This book is designed to make learning 1-2-3 *easy*. This book helps the beginning 1-2-3 user perform basic operations. By following the step-by-step instructions, you can learn how to take advantage of 1-2-3's functions and capabilities.

You don't need to worry that your knowledge of computers or 1-2-3 is too limited to use the program well. This book will teach you all that you need to know.

You don't need to worry that you might do something wrong and ruin a worksheet or the computer. This book points out mistakes that you might make and shows you how to avoid them. This book explains how to escape from a situation when you change your mind during a procedure.

Reading this book builds your confidence. It shows you what steps are necessary to get a particular job done.

How This Book Is Organized

This book is designed with you, the beginner, in mind. The book is divided into several parts, including

- Introduction
- The Basics
- Task/Review
- Reference

The Introduction explains how the book is set up and how you can use it.

The next part, The Basics, outlines general information about your computer and its keyboard layout. This part explains basic concepts such as moving around within your worksheets, selecting commands, and understanding the screen display.

The main part of this book, Task/Review, tells you how to perform specific tasks. Each Task includes numbered steps that tell you the keys to press to complete a specific sample exercise. Before and After pictures of the screen illustrate the exercise.

The Reference part contains a glossary of common computer and 1-2-3 terms. This part also contains a quick reference of the most common features of 1-2-3, along with the keystrokes to access these features.

How To Use This Book

This book is set up so that you can use it several different ways:

- You can read the book from start to finish.
- You can start reading at any point in the book.
- You can experiment with one exercise, many exercises, or all exercises.
- You can look up specific tasks that you want to accomplish, such as copying a cell.
- You can flip through the book, looking at the Before and After pictures, to find specific tasks.
- You can read only the exercise, only the review, or both the exercise and review sections. As you learn the program, you might want to follow along with the exercises. After you learn the program, you can refer back to the review part to remind yourself how to perform a certain task.
- You can read any part of the exercises you want. You can read all the text to see both the steps to follow and the explanation of the steps. You can read only the text in red to see the keystrokes to press. You can read only the explanation to understand what happens during a particular step.

Task section

The Task section includes numbered steps that tell you how to accomplish certain tasks such as saving a worksheet or setting column width. The numbered steps walk you through a specific example so that you can learn the task by doing it. Blue text below the numbered steps explains the concept in more detail.

Oops! notes

You may find that you performed a task that you do not want after all. The Oops! notes tell you how to undo each procedure. In addition, The Oops! notes may also explain how to get out of a situation. By showing you how to reverse nearly every procedure or get out of every mode, these notes allow you to use 1-2-3 more confidently.

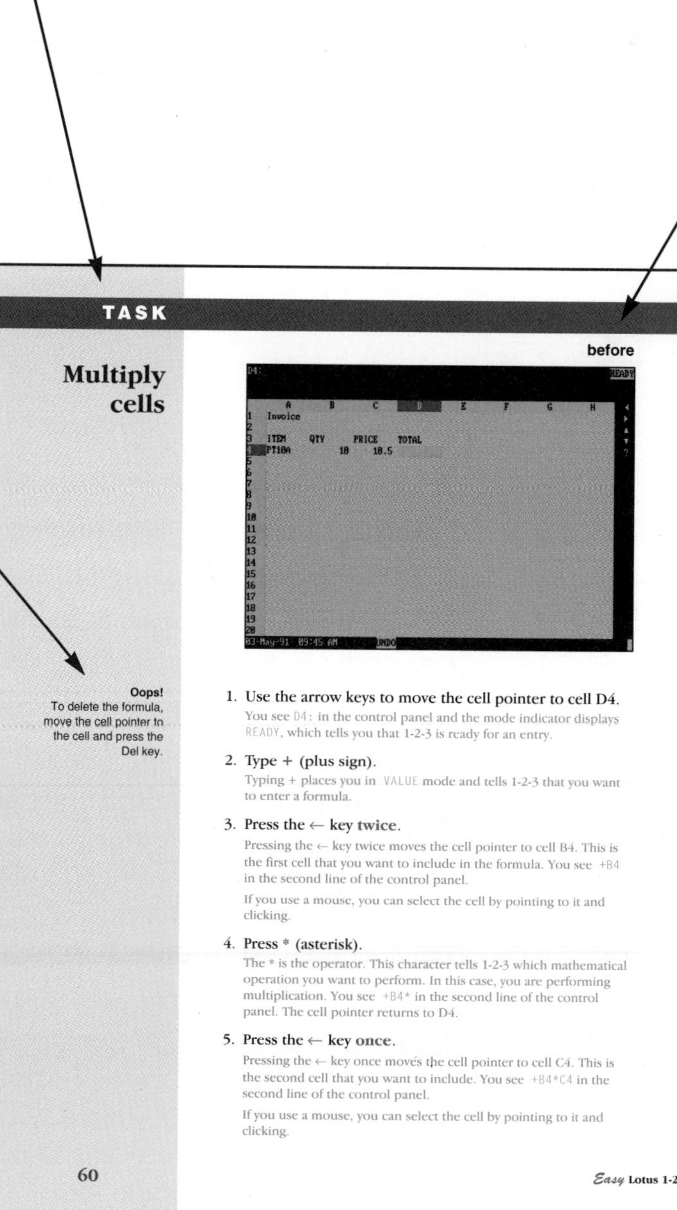

TASK

Multiply cells

before

Oops!
To delete the formula, move the cell pointer to the cell and press the Del key.

1. **Use the arrow keys to move the cell pointer to cell D4.**
   You see D4: in the control panel and the mode indicator displays READY, which tells you that 1-2-3 is ready for an entry.
2. **Type + (plus sign).**
   Typing + places you in VALUE mode and tells 1-2-3 that you want to enter a formula.
3. **Press the ← key twice.**
   Pressing the ← key twice moves the cell pointer to cell B4. This is the first cell that you want to include in the formula. You see +B4 in the second line of the control panel.
   If you use a mouse, you can select the cell by pointing to it and clicking.
4. **Press * (asterisk).**
   The * is the operator. This character tells 1-2-3 which mathematical operation you want to perform. In this case, you are performing multiplication. You see +B4* in the second line of the control panel. The cell pointer returns to D4.
5. **Press the ← key once.**
   Pressing the ← key once moves the cell pointer to cell C4. This is the second cell that you want to include. You see +B4*C4 in the second line of the control panel.
   If you use a mouse, you can select the cell by pointing to it and clicking.

60

Easy Lotus 1-2-3

Before and After Illustrations

Each task includes Before and After illustrations that show how the computer screen will look before and after you follow the numbered steps in the Task sections.

Other notes

Each task contains other short notes that tell you a little more about each procedure. These notes define terms, explain other options, and refer you to other sections when applicable.

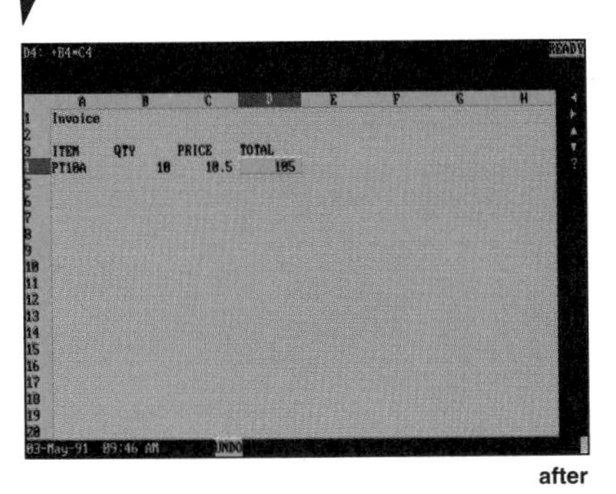

after

Why use a formula?
A formula references a cell's contents, not a fixed value. Therefore, when you change the values in cells, the formula's result automatically adjusts and recalculates.

6. Press **Enter**.

   Pressing Enter tells 1-2-3 that you are finished with the formula. You see the results of the formula (105) in cell D4. You see the formula +B4*C4 in the control panel.

   This formula multiplies the quantity by the price.

REVIEW

To multiply cells

1. Move the cell pointer to the cell in which you want to enter the multiplication formula.
2. Type +.
3. Type or point to the first value that you want to include.
4. Type *.
5. Type or point to the second value that you want to include.
6. Continue typing * and pointing to values until the formula contains all the values that you want.
7. Press **Enter**.

Entering and Editing Data 61

Review section

After you learn a procedure by following a specific example, you can refer to the Review section for a quick summary of the task. The Review section gives you the more generic steps for completing a task so that you can apply those steps to your own work. You can use these steps as a quick reference to refresh your memory about how to perform procedures.

How To Follow an Exercise

1-2-3 is flexible because it enables you to perform a task many different ways. For consistency, this book makes certain assumptions about how your computer is set up and how you use 1-2-3. As you follow each exercise, keep the following key points in mind:

- This book assumes that you followed the basic installation. This book assumes that you have installed a text and graphics printer and that you have not changed any program defaults.
- This book assumes that you use the keyboard—that is, you access the menu by pressing the / (forward slash) key and typing the appropriate command letter. Remember that you can also access commands using the mouse.
- In the exercise sections, this book assumes that you are starting from the Before screen. If this screen contains any data, you should type the text shown in this screen.
- This book shows the screens in color. Your screens may appear in black and white or in different colors.
- Only the Before and After screens are illustrated. Screens are not shown for every step within an exercise.
- Each exercise is independent. That is, you don't have to complete any preceding exercises to follow along with the exercise that you want. If you do follow the exercises from start to finish, you have to erase (or clear) the current worksheet and then create a new file for each exercise. See *TASK: Erase a worksheet* for more information.
- As the tasks get more complex, the examples also become more complex. In some examples, the columns have been widened and the cells formatted.

Where To Get More Help

This book does not cover every 1-2-3 feature or every way to complete a task. This book is geared toward the beginning reader—a reader who wants just the basics. This reader isn't ready for advanced features such as using statistical functions or creating and formatting graphs. This book covers just the most common, basic features.

As you become more comfortable, you may need a more detailed reference book. Que offers several 1-2-3 books to suit your needs:

Using 1-2-3 for DOS Release 2.3, Special Edition

1-2-3 for DOS Release 2.3 QuickStart

1-2-3 for DOS Release 2.3 Quick Reference

Also of interest:

Que's Computer User's Dictionary, 2nd Edition

Introduction to Personal Computers

The Basics

Understanding Your Computer System

Using Your Keyboard

Understanding Key Terms

Understanding the Worksheet Screen

Entering Data

Selecting a Command

Selecting a Range

Saving and Retrieving Your Work

Understanding Your Computer System

Your computer system is made up of these basic parts:

- The system unit
- The monitor
- The keyboard
- The floppy disk drive(s)
- The hard disk drive

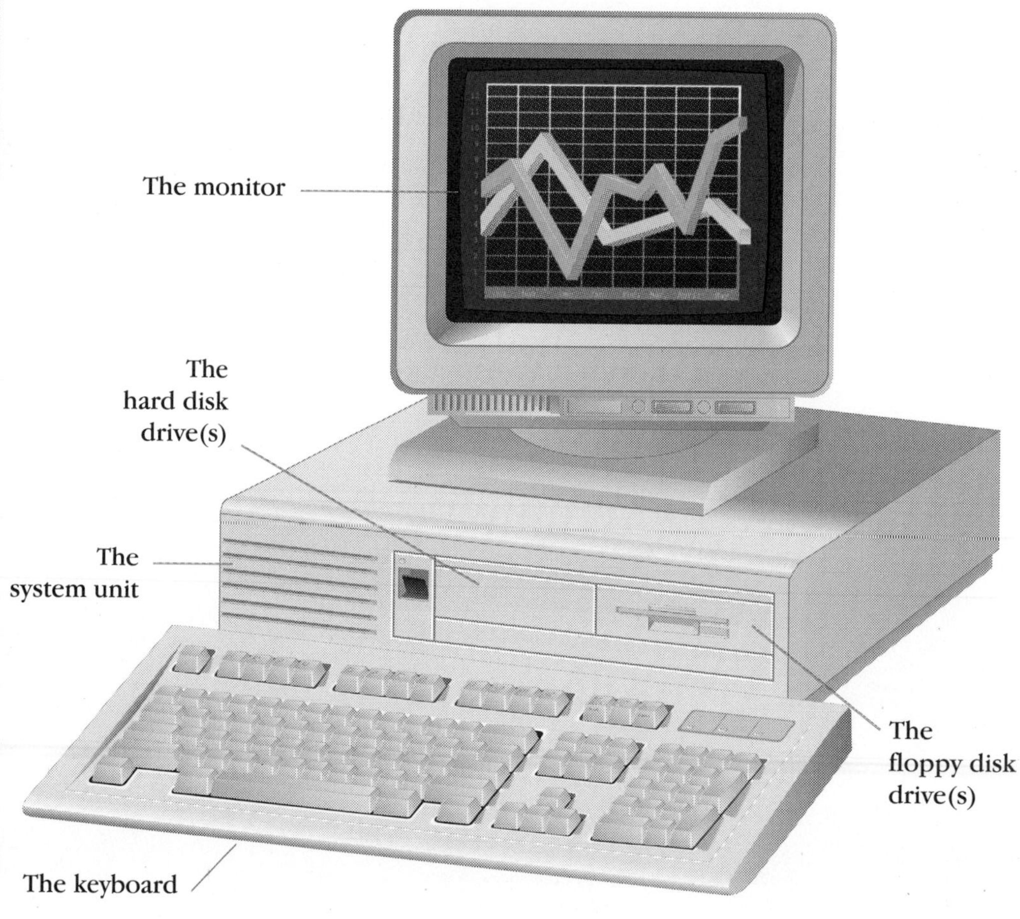

You may also have a mouse and a printer.

System Unit. The system unit is the box that holds all the electrical components of your computer. (The size of the system unit varies.) Somewhere on this box you will find an On switch. (The location of the On switch varies.) To use your computer, you must flip on this switch.

Monitor. The monitor displays on-screen what you type on the keyboard. Your monitor may have a separate On switch. Turn on this switch, also.

Keyboard. You use the keyboard to communicate with the computer. You use it to type text and issue commands. You type on the keyboard just as you do on a regular typewriter. A keyboard also has special keys that you use. (Different computers have different keyboards.) These keys are discussed in the section *Using Your Keyboard*.

Floppy Disk Drive. The floppy disk drive is the door into your computer. It enables you to put information into the computer and place it on the hard drive and to take information from the computer and place it on a floppy disk.

Hard Disk Drive. A hard disk drive stores the programs and files with which you work.

Printer. The printer gives you a paper copy of your on-screen work. To print your documents, you need to attach and install a printer. Installing a printer in 1-2-3 tells the program what type of printer you are using.

Mouse. A mouse is a pointing device that lets you move the cell pointer on-screen, as well as perform other tasks. A mouse is optional; you don't need a mouse to run 1-2-3.

Using Your Keyboard

A computer keyboard is just like a typewriter, only a keyboard has these additional keys:

- Function keys
- Arrow keys
- Other special keys

These keys are located in different places on different keyboards. For example, sometimes the function keys are located across the top of the keyboard. Sometimes they are located on the left side of the keyboard.

Your keyboard also may have a separate numeric keypad. You can use this keypad to move the cell pointer or to enter numbers. See the section *Entering Numbers with the Numeric Keypad*.

For the following keyboard examples, this book uses the Enhanced keyboard. Your keyboard has the same keys, although they might be in a different location. You can familiarize yourself with the keyboard by reading the names on the keys.

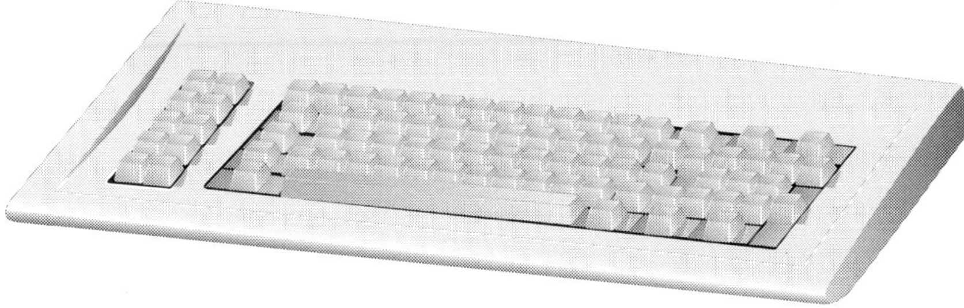

Original PC Keyboard

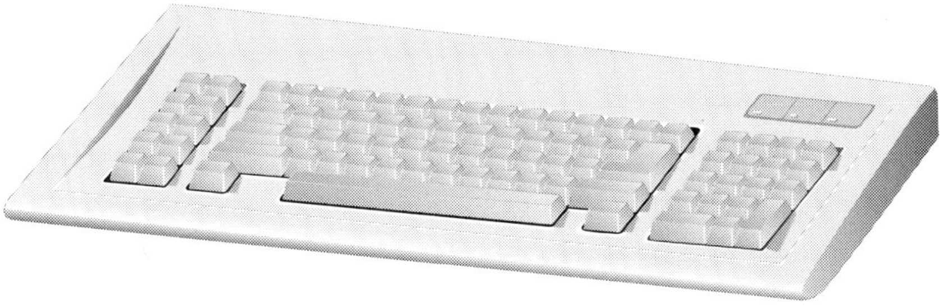

AT Keyboard

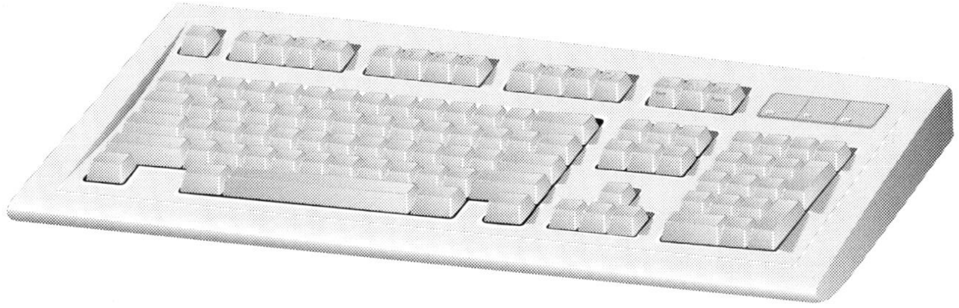

Enhanced Keyboard

Using the Forward Slash and Esc Keys

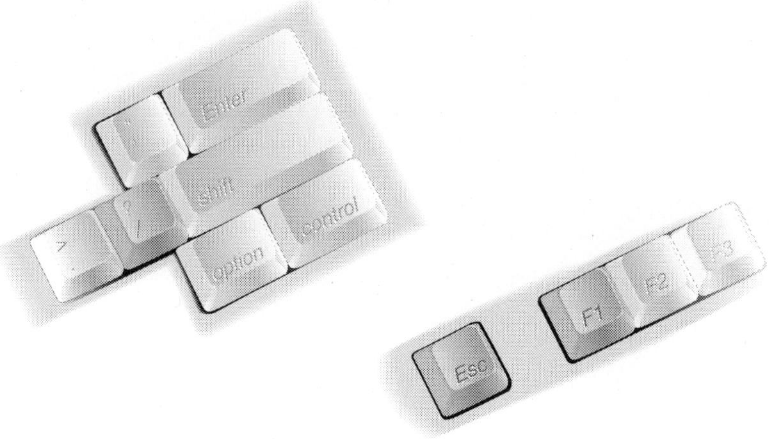

When using 1-2-3, you use these two important keys:

- / (forward slash) key
- Esc key

The / (forward slash) key displays a list of menu commands in the control panel. You select a command by typing the first letter of the command that you want. For example, type /W to select the Worksheet command. See the section *Selecting a Command* for more information.

The Esc key is the "back out" key. You can press this key to escape from most situations. For example, you can press the Esc key to cancel a menu command or to back out of a procedure. Sometimes you may have to press the Esc key several times to back out of a situation completely.

Using the Function Keys

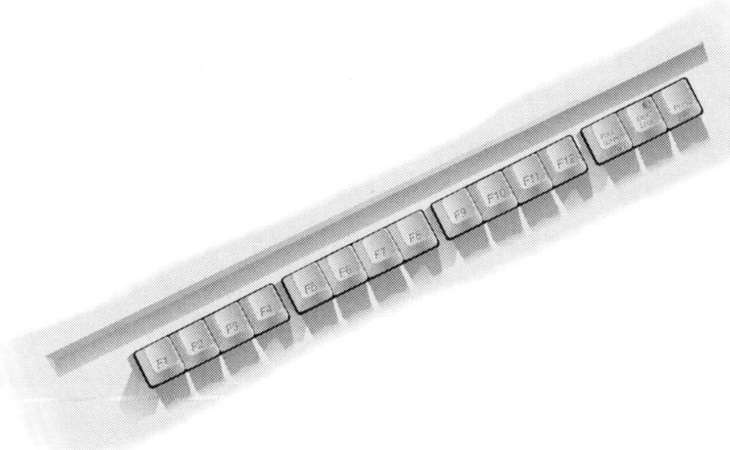

You can access some commands using function keys rather than using the menu. The Enhanced keyboard has 12 function keys labeled F1 through F12. You use the function keys to tell the computer to perform certain commands. For example, pressing the F1 key tells 1-2-3 to display a help screen.

To access some features, you press another key with the function key. For example, to use Undo, you use the Alt-F4 key combination. In this book, a key combination is noted with a hyphen. Press and hold the first key, then press the second key. For this example, you would press and hold the Alt key and then press the F4 key.

Using the Help and Undo Keys

When using 1-2-3, you often use

- The F1 key
- The Alt-F4 key combination

The F1 key is the Help key. Press this key to get on-line help about a particular feature. See *TASK: Get help* in the Task/Review part for more information.

Alt-F4 is the Undo key combination. This key combination enables you to undo some operations. See *TASK: Use Undo* for more information.

Troubleshooting List

When you find yourself in a place in 1-2-3 that you do not want to be, remember the keys and key combination just discussed (/, Esc, F1, and Alt-F4).

You can use these troubleshooting tips when in 1-2-3:

- To back out of a menu, press the Esc key until you return to the worksheet.
- If you see a prompt and don't know how to respond to it, press the Esc key until you return to the worksheet.
- If you get an error message, press the Esc key to clear it. You then can do whatever is necessary to correct the error.
- If you change your mind after performing an operation, press the Alt-F4 key combination to undo the operation.
- If you accidentally delete data, press the Alt-F4 key combination immediately to restore the deleted text.
- If you cannot remember how to perform a task, press the F1 key. You see the Help index; you can use this index to find and display help about a topic. See *TASK: Get help*.

Moving the Cell Pointer

You use the arrow keys to move the cell pointer on-screen. Here is a list of the most common keys and key combinations:

To move	*Press*
To the first cell in the worksheet	Home
One cell right	→
One cell left	←
One row up	↑
One row down	↓
One screen left	Ctrl-← or Shift-Tab
One screen right	Ctrl-→ or Tab
One screen up	PgUp
One screen down	PgDn

Be careful! Don't press the Tab key to move to the next cell. Pressing the Tab key moves the cell pointer one screen to the right rather than one cell. If you suddenly see a blank screen, it may be because you have pressed the Tab key. Press Shift-Tab to move back one screen.

Entering Numbers with the Numeric Keypad

You may have two sets of arrow keys: one that you use to move only the cell pointer and one to move the cell pointer or to enter numbers. The second set is called the numeric keypad. These keys have both numbers and arrows on them. You can use the numeric keypad to enter numbers.

To use the numeric keypad, press the Num Lock key. (Look for the words *Num Lock* or something similar on the key.) This key is a toggle, which means that it switches back and forth between numbers and arrows each time you press it.

If you press the Num Lock key once, the keypad turns on the number lock and you can use the numbers. Press the key again to turn off the number lock and use the arrows on the keypad.

If you press an arrow key to move the cell pointer and numbers type on-screen instead, you have left the Num Lock option turned on. Press the Num Lock key to turn it off.

1-2-3 displays `NUM` in the status line when the Num Lock key is on.

Editing Data

As you edit, you use four important editing keys:

- The Enter key
- The Del (or Delete) key
- The F2 key
- The Backspace key

To enter data in a cell, move the cell pointer to that cell, type the entry, and press Enter. Pressing Enter confirms the entry and moves the data from the input line to the cell. You can also press the arrow keys to enter the data. See the tasks on entering text, numbers, dates, and so on for more information on entering data.

The Del key clears an entry. To clear a cell, move the cell pointer to that cell and press the Del key. See *TASK: Erase a cell.*

To edit a cell, press the F2 key and then use the arrow keys to move to the characters that you want to change. (You can also use the Backspace key to erase characters.) Make your changes and press Enter. For more information on editing a cell, see *TASK: Edit a cell*.

Understanding Key Terms

To use 1-2-3, you should understand the following key terms:

cell. The intersection of any column and row. Each cell in a worksheet has a unique address.

cell coordinates. The address formed by combining the column and row locations into one description. For example, A8 describes the intersection of column A and row 8.

cell pointer. A highlighted rectangle that indicates the active cell. The cell pointer shows where data is entered or where a range begins.

directory. An index to the files stored on disk or a list of files. A directory is similar to a file cabinet; you can group files together in directories.

file. The various individual reports, memos, databases, and worksheets that you store on your hard drive (or disk) for future use.

formula. An entry that performs a calculation on two or more values or series of values. A formula can reference cells or values. +1+4 is a formula, as is +B1+B2. The second formula adds the contents of cells B1 and B2.

function. A built-in formula that is included with 1-2-3. Functions perform specialized calculations for you, such as loan payments.

label. A text entry.

menu. A list of 1-2-3 commands that appears in the control panel when you press the / (forward slash) key.

range. A rectangular area of data. A range can be a cell, a row, a column, or any combination of contiguous columns and rows. After you select a range, you can perform different actions such as copy, erase, enhance, and so on. The Task/Review part covers range operations.

range address. The method that 1-2-3 uses to identify a range. The first element in the range address is the location of the uppermost left cell in the range; the second element is the location of the lowermost right cell. The two elements are separated by two periods. For example, the range A1..C3 includes the cells A1, A2, A3, B1, B2, B3, C1, C2, and C3.

value. A number, formula, date, or time entry.

worksheet. The blank screen that appears when you start 1-2-3. A worksheet is also all the data and formatting information that you enter on-screen. 1-2-3 and your operating system keep track of worksheets by storing them in files on disk.

Understanding the Worksheet Screen

After you start the program, you see a blank worksheet screen. Look at the worksheet area and then note some other important screen areas. If you want to start the program and follow along, see *TASK: Start 1-2-3.* This is the first task in the Task/Review portion of this book.

The Worksheet Area

The main part of the worksheet screen is the worksheet area. A worksheet is a grid of columns and rows. A 1-2-3 worksheet has 256 columns and 8,192 rows.

Columns read from top to bottom and are numbered with letters (A-Z, AB-AZ, and so on through IV).

Rows read across the worksheet and are numbered 1 through 8192.

A cell is the intersection of a column and row. The cell pointer, which is a highlighted bar, indicates the active cell.

Use the arrow keys to move the cell pointer to a different cell.

The Control Panel

The first three lines of the screen display important information. These lines are called the control panel. You see different items in the control panel.

When you press the / (forward slash) key to access 1-2-3 commands, you see a list of commands in the second line of the control panel; the first command is highlighted. The third line lists the subcommands for the highlighted command. For example, if Worksheet is highlighted in the second line, the third line displays Worksheet commands.

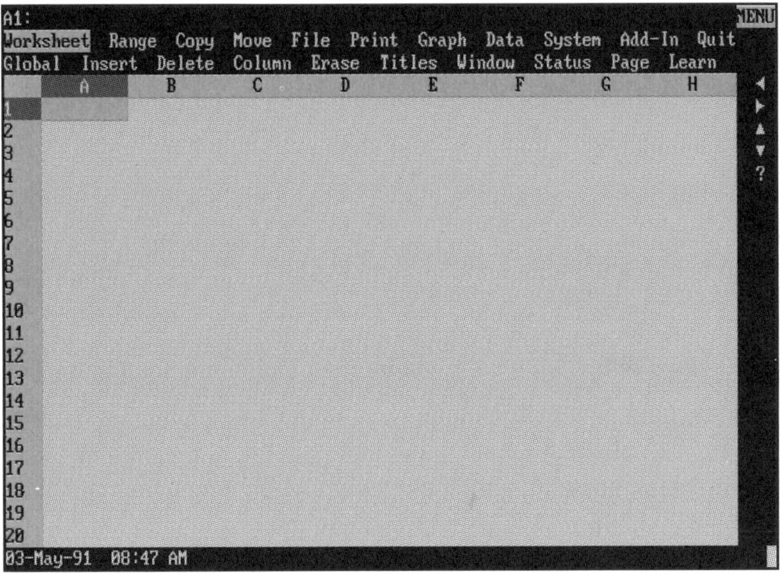

When you enter data, you see information about the current cell in the control panel. You see the cell address. If you have entered something in the cell, you also see this entry. And if you have formatted the line, you see codes that indicate the format change.

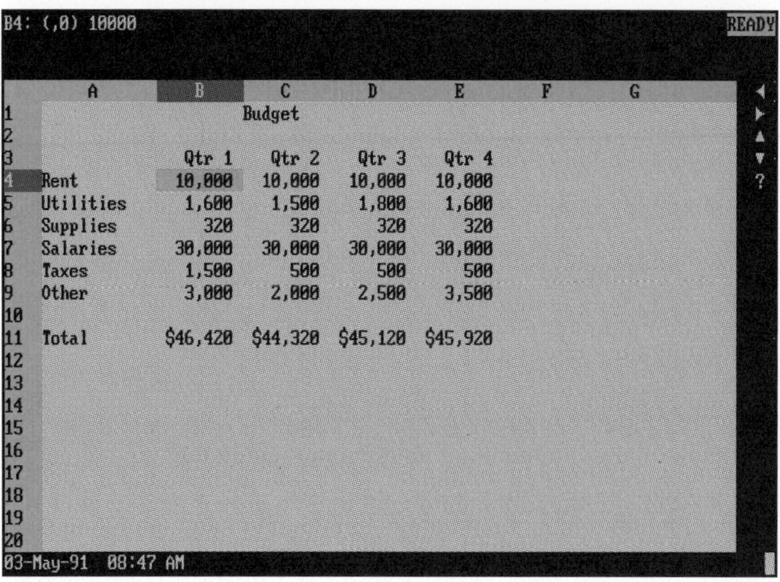

The control panel also displays mode information. For instance, the mode indicator `READY` tells you that 1-2-3 is ready for your entry. Refer to *Using 1-2-3 for DOS, Release 2.3,* Special Edition, for a complete list of status and mode indicators.

Entering Data

1-2-3 accepts two types of data as valid entries: labels and values. A label is a text entry. A value can be a number, formula, date, or time.

The first character that you type tells 1-2-3 how to interpret the entry. If you type a number, 1-2-3 expects a value. If you type an alphabetic character (A-Z), 1-2-3 expects a label.

Entering a Label

To enter a label (text), position the cell pointer in the cell where you want to add the text, type the entry, and press Enter. 1-2-3 precedes labels with a prefix. The prefix tells

1-2-3 that the entry is text and indicates how the entry is to be aligned. The default alignment is left, which is indicated by an apostrophe (').

Use labels as row and column headings and for all text entries (such as names, titles, and so on). You should enter numbers (such as phone numbers, addresses, social security numbers, and so on) as a label. These entries are text, as opposed to values that you would use in a formula.

To enter a number as a label (for instance, a phone number), you must type an apostrophe (') first, then type the entry. If you type just the number, 1-2-3 interprets the entry as a value. For example, if you type *555-3756*, 1-2-3 interprets the entry as 555 *minus* 3756. 1-2-3 evaluates this formula and displays the result (in this example, –3201) in the cell instead of the number.

See *TASK: Enter text* for more information.

Entering a Value

To enter a value, position the cell pointer in the cell you want, type the value, and press Enter. To type a negative number, type a minus sign before the number. See *TASK: Enter a number* for more information.

Entering Other Values

You use special methods to enter dates, times, and formulas. These entries are also considered values.

See *TASK: Enter a date* and *TASK: Enter a time* for information on dates and times.

To enter a formula, see *TASK: Add cells*, *TASK: Subtract cells*, *TASK: Multiply cells*, *TASK: Divide two cells*, *TASK: Use the @SUM function*, and *TASK: Calculate an average*.

Selecting a Command

You access commands through 1-2-3's menu system. Start by pressing the / (forward slash) key to enter MENU mode. When you press the / key, commands are listed in the second line of the control panel. The first command, Worksheet, is highlighted.

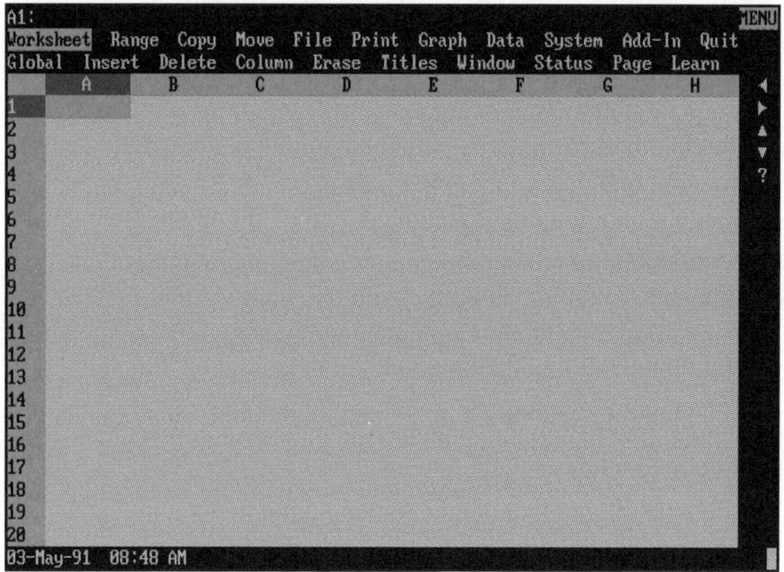

Next type the first letter in the menu command. For example, type W to select the Worksheet command. (Because this command is already highlighted, you can also press Enter to select this command.) You can also use the arrow keys to move the menu pointer to the command you want to open and then press Enter.

When you select a command, you see a list of commands in the next menu. To select one of these commands, type the first letter. For instance, type E to select Erase. You can also use the arrow keys to move the menu pointer to the option; then press Enter.

Sometimes additional commands are displayed. Access these commands using the procedure just described.

This book combines typing the / (forward slash) key with the key letter. For example, suppose that a step says "Type /FR." You would press the / key to display the menu, type F to select File, and type R to select Retrieve.

You can also use the mouse to select menu commands. Move the mouse pointer to the control panel to access the menu. Then move the mouse pointer to the desired menu option and click the left button.

If you don't see the command that you want; or if you want to return to the worksheet without selecting a command, press the Esc key until the menu disappears and 1-2-3 displays READY in the control panel.

Selecting a Range

A range is any rectangular section of the worksheet; it can be a cell, a column, a row, or a combination of contiguous columns and rows. You can perform many actions on a range, such as copy a range, move a range, format a range, and so on. These tasks are covered in the Task/Review part of the book.

One of the most important tasks to learn is how to select a range. You can select a range several different ways:

- Point to the range
- Use the mouse
- Type the range address

Pointing to the Range

When you issue a command that you can apply to a range, you are prompted to specify the range. In this case, press the . (period) key to anchor the first cell and to enter `POINT` mode. Then use the arrow keys to highlight the range that you want. Press Enter to accept the range.

Using the Mouse

To select a range with the mouse, move the mouse pointer to the first cell in the range, press and hold the mouse button, and drag the mouse diagonally to highlight the cells that you want in the range.

Typing the Range Address

You can also type the range address when prompted. The range address consists of the upper leftmost cell, two periods, and the lower rightmost cell.

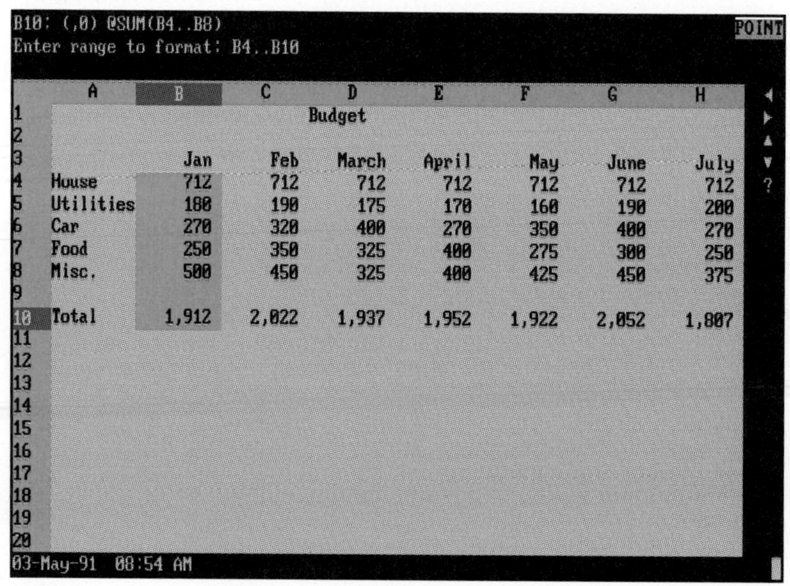

Saving and Retrieving Your Work

All your work is stored temporarily in memory, which is like having a shopping list in your head. Until you commit the list to paper, you may forget some or all the items. The same is true with 1-2-3. Until you save the worksheet, you can lose all or part of your work.

Saving the worksheet doesn't commit it to paper like the shopping list. Saving the worksheet saves the data to your disk. Then when you need the worksheet again, you can retrieve it from the disk.

1-2-3 does not save your work automatically; you need to save it yourself. You should save every 5 or 10 minutes.

You have these choices when you save a document:

When you want to	*Refer to*
Save a worksheet that you have not saved	*TASK: Save a worksheet for the first time*
Retrieve a worksheet that you have saved	*TASK: Retrieve a worksheet*
Save a worksheet that you have saved once already	*TASK: Save a worksheet again*
Save a copy of a worksheet under a new name and keep the original	*TASK: Save a worksheet with a new name*
Clear the screen to start a new worksheet	*TASK: Erase a worksheet*
Clear the screen and abandon the worksheet on-screen; return to the previous version (if you have saved) or lose the current version (if you haven't saved)	*TASK: Abandon the worksheet*

Task/Review

Entering and Editing Data

Managing Files

Formatting the Worksheet

Advanced Editing

Printing and Enhancing the Worksheet

Alphabetical Listing of Tasks

Entering and Editing Data

This section covers the following tasks:

Start 1-2-3

Exit 1-2-3

Get help

Turn on Undo

Enter text

Enter a number

Enter a date

Enter a time

Add cells

Subtract cells

Multiply cells

Divide two cells

Overwrite a cell

Edit a cell

Erase a cell

Copy a cell

Move a cell

Go to a specific cell

Use Undo

TASK

Start 1-2-3

before

Oops!
If the program doesn't start, be sure that you specified the correct directory for the program files in step 4. You may have installed the program in a different directory.

1. **Turn on the computer and monitor.**

   Every computer has a different location for its On/Off switch. Check the side, the front, and the back of your computer. Your monitor also may have a separate On/Off switch. If so, you also need to turn on the monitor.

2. **If necessary, respond to the prompts for date and time.**

   When you first turn on the computer, some systems ask you to enter the current date and time. (Many of the newer models enter the time and date automatically. If you aren't prompted for these entries, don't worry.)

   If the computer prompts you, type the current date and press Enter. Then type the current time and press Enter. The computer then adds the correct date and time to any files that you save. You should complete this step so that your file information is complete.

3. **Install the program.**

   To use 1-2-3, the program must be installed on your hard drive. You only need to install the program once. Follow the installation procedures outlined in the 1-2-3 manual that came with the software. This book assumes that the program is installed in the \123r23 directory on the C hard drive.

4. **Type cd\123r23.**

   This command tells the computer to change to the 1-2-3 directory. This directory is named *123r23* and contains the 1-2-3 program files; these files are needed to start and run the program.

after

5. Press **Enter**.

   Pressing Enter places you in the 1-2-3 directory. You see the prompt `C:\123r23>`.

6. Type **123**.

   Typing *123* starts the program.

7. Press **Enter**.

REVIEW

To start 1-2-3

1. Turn on your computer and monitor.
2. Respond to the prompts for the date and time, if necessary.
3. Make sure that you have installed the program.
4. Type **cd\123r23**.
5. Press **Enter**.
6. Type **123**.
7. Press **Enter**.

TASK

Exit 1-2-3

before

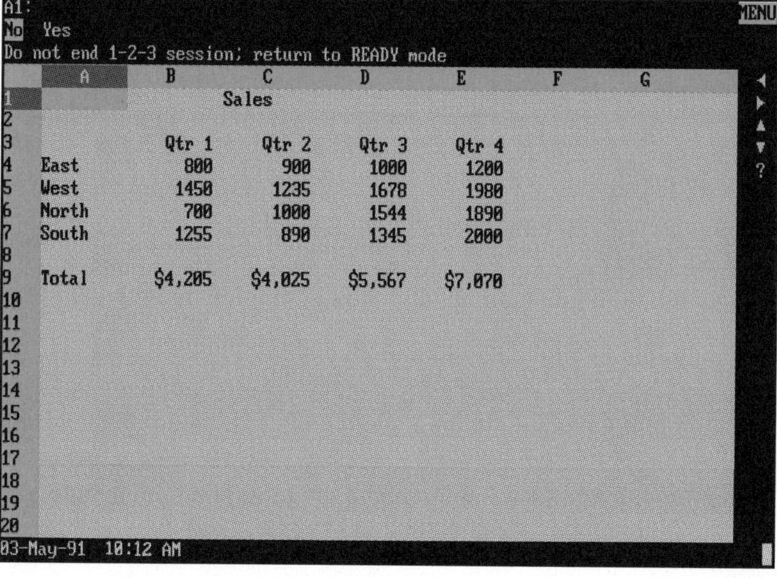

Oops!
If you want to restart the program after you have exited, type *123* at the `C:\123R23>` prompt.

1. **Save the worksheet.**

   See any of the tasks that discuss saving the worksheet in the next section, *Managing Files*.

2. **Type /Q.**

   Typing /Q selects the Quit command. You see a prompt that offers two choices: No and Yes.

3. **Type Y.**

   Typing Y confirms that you want to quit the program. If you have already saved the worksheet, you return to DOS.

   If you have not saved the worksheet, or if you have made any changes since you last saved the worksheet, 1-2-3 beeps and you see the prompt `WORKSHEET CHANGES NOT SAVED! End 1-2-3 anyway?`. Type Y to quit; type N to return to the worksheet.

after

REVIEW

To exit 1-2-3

1. Save the worksheet.
2. Type /Q to select the Quit command.
3. Type Y.

Get help

before

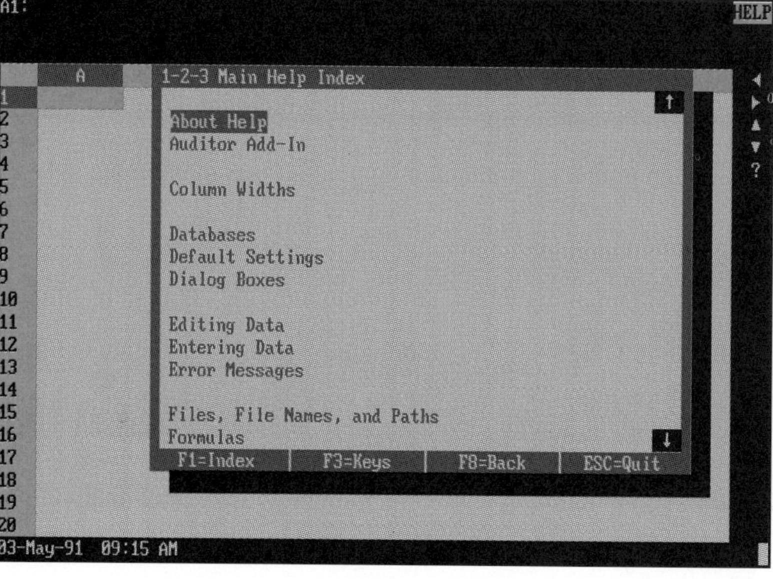

Oops!
To exit help, press the Esc key.

1. **Press F1.**

   F1 is the Help key. You see the 1-2-3 Main Help Index.

2. **Press the ↓ key six times.**

   Pressing the ↓ key six times moves the cell pointer through the topics and highlights the topic *Editing Data*. This topic displays help on editing data in 1-2-3.

3. **Press Enter.**

   Pressing Enter confirms your choice. You see information on-screen about editing your work.

4. **Press Esc.**

   Pressing the Esc key exits Help. You return to the worksheet.

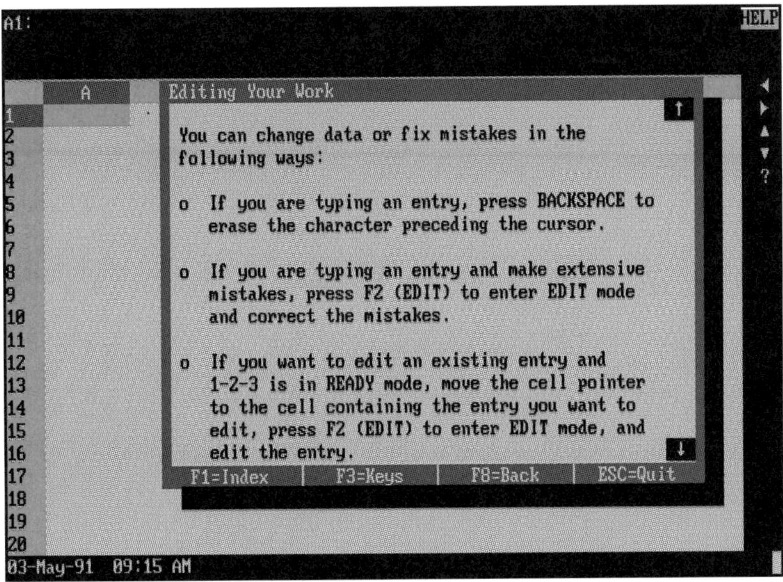

after

REVIEW

To get help

1. Press **F1** (Help).
2. Highlight the topic that you want.
3. Press **Enter**.
4. Press **Esc** to exit.

Return to the index
If you press the ↓ key the wrong number of times, press the F1 key to return to the index.

TASK

Turn on Undo

before

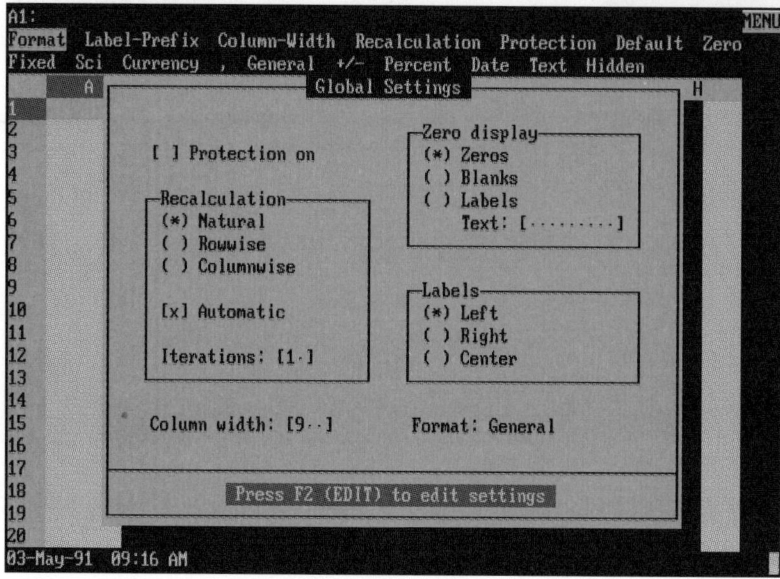

Oops!
If you make a wrong menu choice, press the Esc key until you return to the worksheet; then start over again.

1. Type **/WG**.

   Typing /WG selects the Worksheet Global command. You see the Global Settings dialog box. In the control panel, you see a list of options that you can specify.

   Undo may already be enabled (or turned on) on your machine. To be certain that it is turned on, follow these instructions.

2. Type **D**.

   Typing D selects Default. You see the Default Settings dialog box in the middle of the screen and a list of command choices in the control panel.

3. Type **O**.

   Typing O selects Other. You see a list of other settings to change.

4. Type **U**.

   Typing U selects Undo. You see two choices: Enable and Disable.

5. Type **E**.

   Typing E selects Enable. Notice that in the dialog box, `Undo on` has a check mark next to it. This means that Undo is enabled or turned on for this work session.

   If an error message appears, your computer may not have enough memory. For instance, if you have attached an add-in (see *TASK: Attach Wysiwyg*), you may not be able to run Undo. Detach all add-ins and try again. See your 1-2-3 manual or *Using 1-2-3 for DOS Release 2.3,* Special Edition, for more information on memory.

after

6. Type **U**.

   Typing U updates and saves the settings for future work sessions. Undo is then turned on whenever you start the program.

7. Type **Q**.

   Typing Q closes the menu and returns you to the worksheet. You see `UNDO` in the status line at the bottom of the screen.

The effects of Undo
The Undo feature uses memory and may slow down the computer some. Without Undo, however, you cannot reverse changes in the worksheet.

REVIEW

To turn on Undo

1. Type **/WG** to select the Worksheet Global command.
2. Type **DO** to select Default Other.
3. Type **UE** to select Undo Enable.
4. Type **U** to select Update.
5. Type **Q** to close the menu.

Use Undo
To use the Undo feature, see *TASK: Use Undo.*

Enter text

before

Oops!
To delete a text entry, position the cell pointer in the cell and press the Del key.

1. Press the → key **three times**.

   Pressing the → key three times moves the cell pointer to cell D1. The active cell on a worksheet appears as a highlighted rectangle.

   Each cell in a spreadsheet has a unique address. A cell address is formed by combining the column and row locations into one description. For example, D1 describes the intersection of column D and row 1.

   You see `D1:` on the first line of the control panel. In the upper right corner, you see the prompt `READY`. This mode indicator means that 1-2-3 is ready to accept an entry.

2. Type **Budget**.

   Budget is the title of your worksheet. The mode indicator changes to `LABEL`, which indicates that you are entering a label (text).

   You see the entry on the second line of the control panel. Before you press Enter, you can use the Backspace key to edit the entry in the control panel.

after

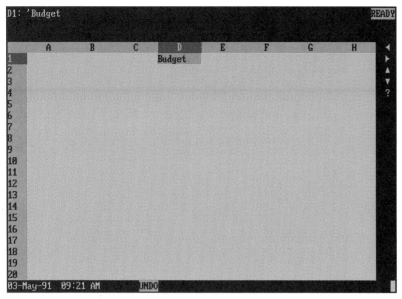

Use the arrow keys
You can press any of the arrow keys to accept an entry and move the cell pointer.

3. Press **Enter**.

   Pressing Enter accepts the entry and enters it into the cell. The cell pointer remains in cell D1. You see the title in the first line of the control panel. The entry is preceded by an apostrophe. An apostrophe tells 1-2-3 that this entry is a label (text), rather than a number or a formula. The row and column headings also may be labels.

   Notice that the entry is left-aligned. This alignment is the default format for labels. To change this format, see the tasks on formatting the worksheet later in this book.

REVIEW

To enter text

1. Move the cell pointer to the cell in which you want to enter text.
2. Type the text.
3. Press **Enter** or **any arrow key**.

Enter a number as a label
To enter a number as a label, you must type an apostrophe first, then type the entry. See *Entering Data* in the preceding part, The Basics.

TASK

Enter a number

before

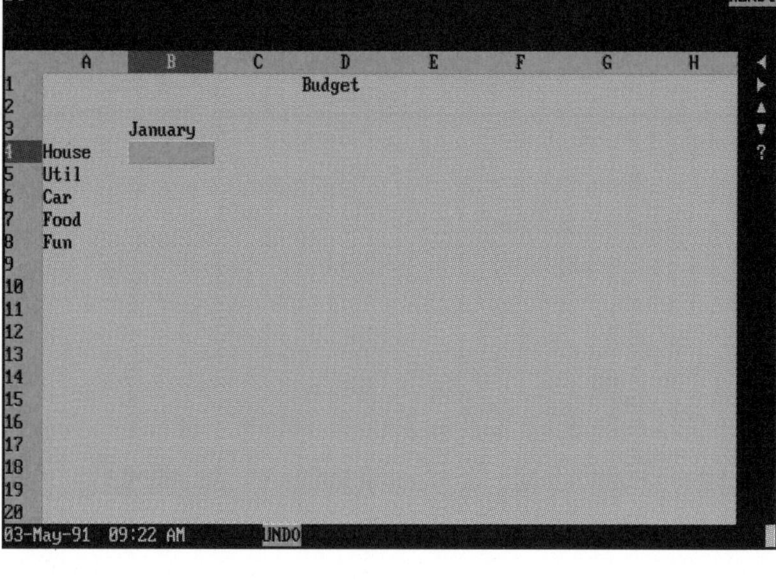

Oops!
To delete a number, position the cell pointer in the cell that you want to erase and press the Del key.

1. Use the arrow keys to move to cell B4.

   You see `B4:` on the first line of the control panel. The mode indicator, `READY`, tells you that 1-2-3 is ready to accept an entry.

2. Type **712**.

   You see `712` on the second line of the control panel. The mode indictor changes to `VALUE` to show that this entry is a value. A value can be a number, a formula, or a date.

   Before you press Enter, you can use the Backspace key to edit the entry in the control panel.

3. Press the ↓ key **once**.

   Pressing the ↓ key accepts the entry, enters the value into the cell, and moves the cell pointer to the next row (cell B5).

   Notice that the entry is right-aligned and that no decimal places, commas, or dollar signs are displayed. This style is the default format for numbers. You can change this format. See the tasks in the *Formatting the Worksheet* section.

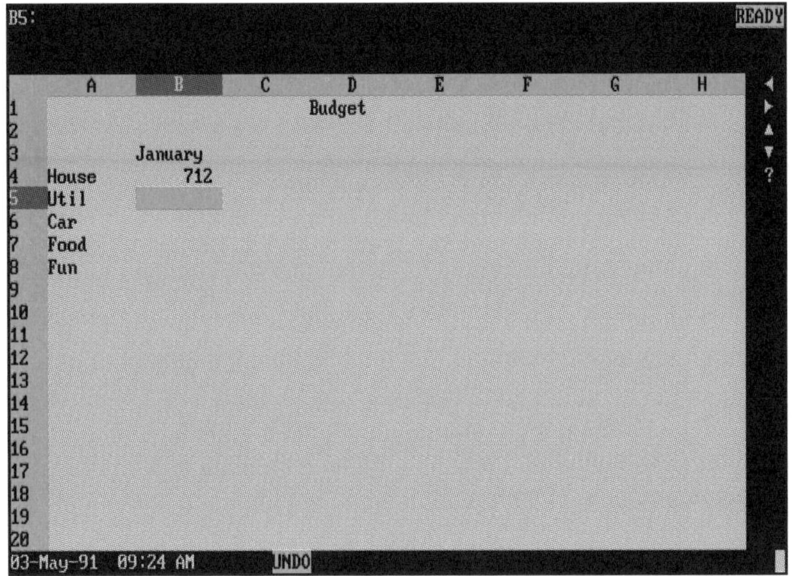

after

Enter a negative number
To enter a negative number, type a – (minus sign). Then type the number.

REVIEW

To enter a number

1. Move the cell pointer to the cell in which you want to enter the number.
2. Type the number.
3. Press **Enter** or **any arrow key**.

TASK

Enter a date

before

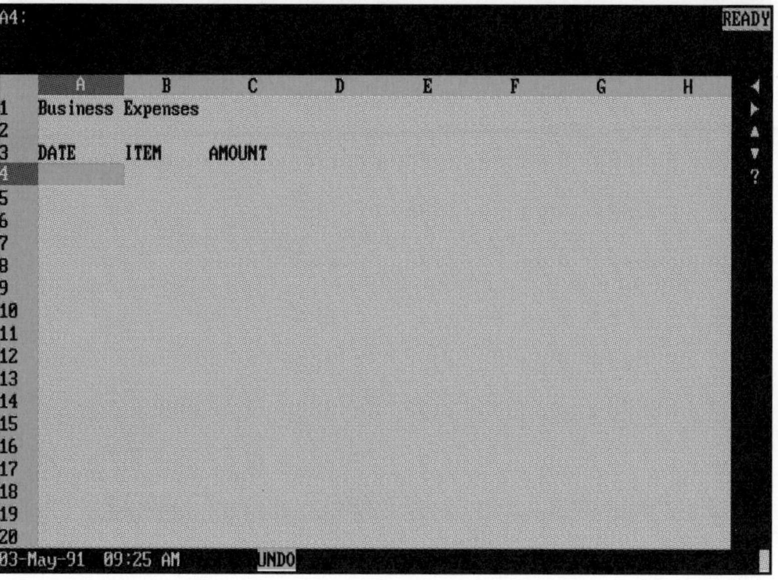

Oops!
If 1-2-3 does not accept your entry, you may not have typed it correctly. Press Esc and start over.

1. **Use the arrow keys to move the cell pointer to cell A4.**
   You see `A4:` on the first line of the control panel. The mode indicator, `READY`, tells you that 1-2-3 is ready to accept an entry.

2. **Type @DATE(91,8,14).**
   1-2-3 treats dates in a particular way. If you type the date without using a special entry method, 1-2-3 tries to enter the date as a value. For example, if you type 8-14-91, 1-2-3 interprets the entry as 8 *minus* 14 *minus* 91. 1-2-3 evaluates the formula and displays the result in the cell.

   You must use a special function to enter dates. @DATE is one function that you can use. Inside the parentheses, you enter the year, the month, and the date. Separate each entry with commas.

3. **Press Enter.**
   Pressing Enter confirms the entry. 1-2-3 translates the function and returns a number—`33464`. This number appears in the cell, and the date function appears in the control panel. 1-2-3 stores dates as serial numbers. The numbering starts with 1 (December 31, 1899) and continues up to the present date. 1-2-3 uses this format so that you can perform mathematical operations on dates, such as subtracting two dates.

4. **Type /RF.**
   Typing /RF selects the Range Format command. You see a list of Format options in the control panel.

5. **Type D.**
   Typing D selects Date. You see a list of date formats in the control panel.

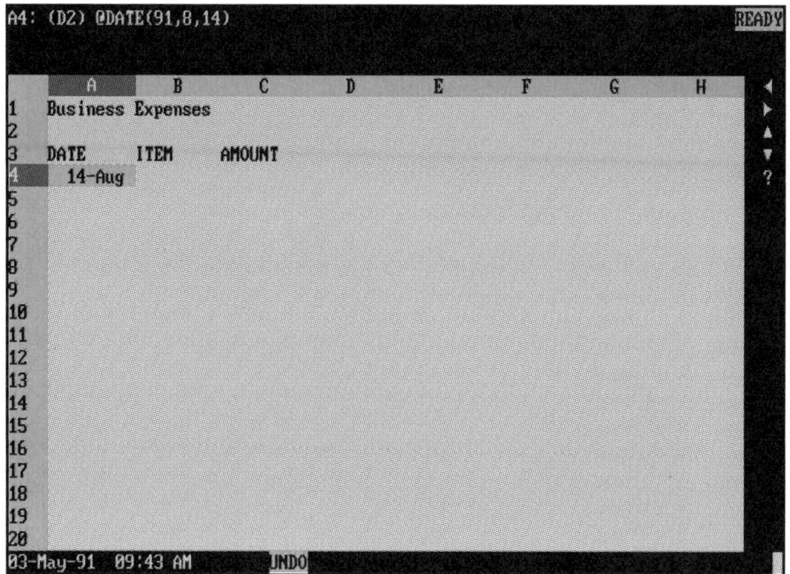

after

Learn more about date formats

For more information on date formats, see *TASK: Format a date.*

6. Type 2.

   Typing 2 selects the date format DD-MMM. You see the prompt `Enter range to format: A4..A4`. A4 is the current cell.

7. Press Enter.

   Pressing Enter tells 1-2-3 to format the current cell. In the cell, you see `14-Aug`, but in the control panel you see the date function.

REVIEW

To enter a date

1. Move the cell pointer to the cell in which you want to enter the date.
2. Type @DATE(*yy,mm,dd*). Substitute the year for *yy*, the month for *mm*, and the day for *dd*.
3. Press Enter.
4. Type /RF to select the Range Format command.
5. Type D to select Date.
6. Select a date format.
7. Point to or type the range address.
8. Press Enter.

Learn more about date functions

For more information on date functions, see *Using 1-2-3 for DOS Release 2.3,* Special Edition.

TASK

Enter a time

before

Oops!
If 1-2-3 beeps and does not accept the entry, you entered it incorrectly. Press Esc and start over.

1. **Use the arrow keys to move the cell pointer to cell C3.**

   You see `C3:` on the first line of the control panel. The mode indicator displays `READY`, which tells you that 1-2-3 is ready to accept an entry.

2. **Type @TIME(8,0,0).**

   1-2-3 treats times in a particular way. If you type the time without using a special entry method, 1-2-3 tries to enter the time as a value. You then receive an error message.

   You must use a special function to enter times. @TIME is one of the functions that you can use. Inside the parentheses, you enter the hour, the minutes, and the seconds.

3. **Press Enter.**

   Pressing Enter confirms the entry. 1-2-3 translates the function and returns a number—`0.333333`. 1-2-3 stores a time as a fraction of a 24-hour period. 1-2-3 uses this format so that you can perform mathematical operations on times, such as subtracting two times.

4. **Type /RF.**

   Typing /RF selects the Range Format command. You see a list of Format options in the control panel.

5. **Type DT.**

   Typing DT selects Date Time. You see a list of time formats in the control panel.

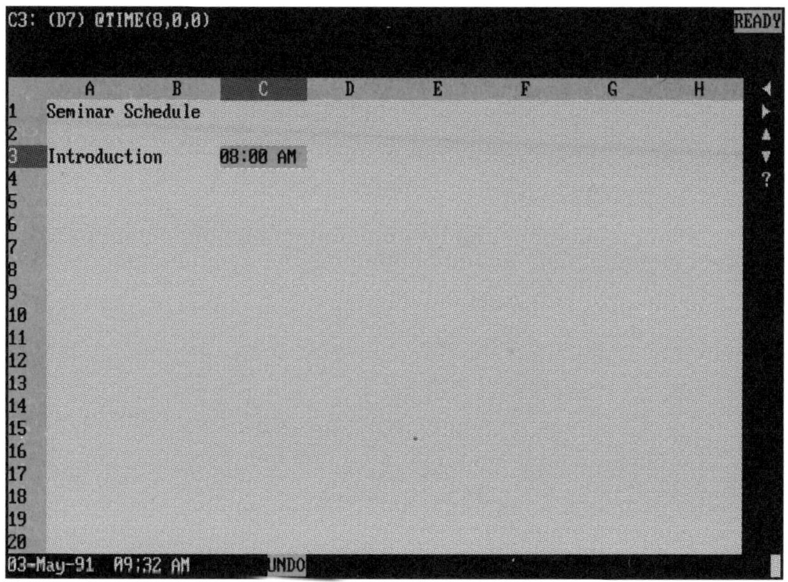

after

6. Type **2**.

   Typing 2 selects the time format HH:MM AM/PM. You see the prompt `Enter range to format: C3..C3`.

7. Press **Enter**.

   Pressing Enter tells 1-2-3 to format the current cell. In the cell, you see `08:00 AM`, but in the control panel you see the time function.

Learn more about time formats
For more information on time formats, see *TASK: Format a time.*

REVIEW

To enter a time

1. Move the cell pointer to the cell in which you want to enter the time.
2. Type **@TIME(*hh,mm,ss*)**. Substitute the hour for *hh*, the minutes for *mm*, and the seconds for *ss*. Use a 24-hour clock.
3. Press **Enter**.
4. Type **/RF** to select the Range Format command.
5. Type **DT** to select Date Time.
6. Select a time format.
7. Specify the range to format.
8. Press **Enter**.

Learn more about time functions
For more information on time functions, see *Using 1-2-3 for DOS Release 2.3,* Special Edition.

TASK

Add cells

before

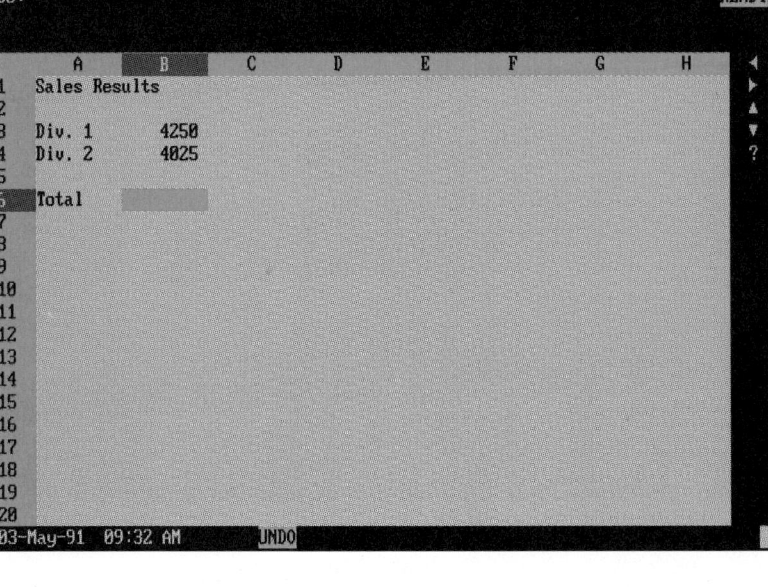

Oops!
To delete the formula, move the cell pointer to the cell and press the Del key.

1. Use the arrow keys to move the cell pointer to cell B6.

   You see `B6:` on the first line of the control panel. The mode indicator displays `READY`, which tells you that 1-2-3 is ready for an entry.

2. Type + (plus sign).

   Typing + places you in `VALUE` mode and tells 1-2-3 that you want to enter a formula.

3. Press the ↑ key **three times**.

   Pressing the ↑ key three times moves the cell pointer to cell B3. This is the first cell that you want to include in the addition formula. You see `+B3` in the second line of the control panel.

   If you use a mouse, you can point to the cell and click. You can also type the cell reference (B3, for example) rather than point to it.

4. Press + (plus sign).

   The + is the operator. This character tells 1-2-3 which mathematical operation you want to perform. In this case, you are performing addition. The cell pointer returns to cell B6.

5. Press the ↑ key **twice**.

   Pressing the ↑ key twice moves the cell pointer to cell B4. This is the second cell that you want to include in your formula. You see `+B3+B4` in the second line of the control panel.

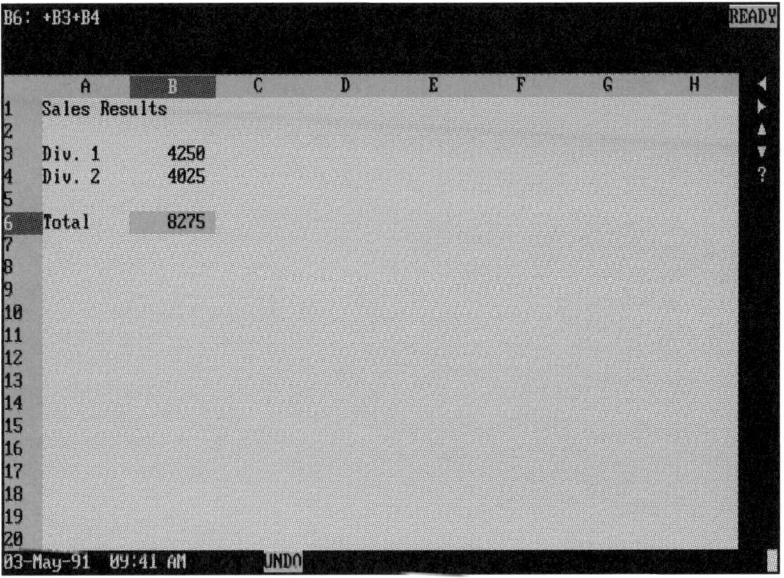

after

If you have a mouse, you can click on cell B4 to select it. You also can type the cell reference.

6. Press **Enter**.

   Pressing Enter tells 1-2-3 that you are finished with the addition formula. You see the results of the formula (8275) in cell B6. In the control panel, you see the formula +B3+B4.

   This formula adds the sales for the two divisions.

Why use a formula?
A formula references a cell's contents, not a fixed value. Therefore, when you change the values in cells, the formula's result automatically adjusts and recalculates.

REVIEW

To add cells

1. Move the cell pointer to the cell in which you want to enter the formula.
2. Type +.
3. Type or point to the first value that you want to add.
4. Type +.
5. Type or point to the second value that you want to add.
6. Continue typing + and pointing to values until the formula includes all the values that you want.
7. Press **Enter**.

Use the @SUM function
You also can use the @SUM function to add values. See *TASK: Use the @SUM function.*

TASK

Subtract cells

before

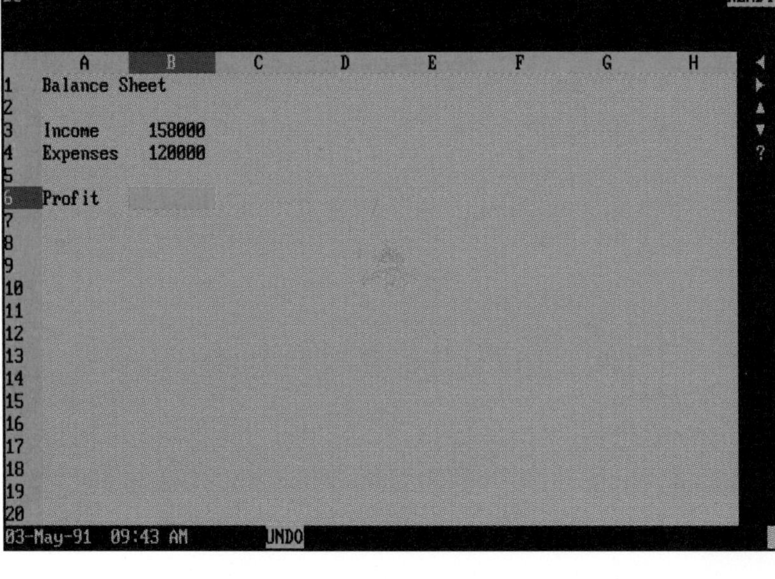

Oops!
To delete a formula, move the cell pointer to the cell and press the Del key.

1. **Use the arrow keys to move the cell pointer to cell B6.**

   You see B6: in the control panel. The mode indicator displays READY, which tells you that 1-2-3 is ready for an entry.

2. **Type + (plus sign).**

   Typing + places you in VALUE mode and tells 1-2-3 that you want to enter a formula. You point to the cells that you want to include in this formula.

3. **Press the ↑ key three times.**

   Pressing the ↑ key three times moves the cell pointer to cell B3. This is the first cell that you want to include in the formula. You see +B3 in the second line of the control panel.

   If you use a mouse, you can select the cell by pointing to it and clicking.

4. **Press – (minus sign).**

   The – is the operator. It tells 1-2-3 which mathematical operation you want to perform. In this case, you are performing subtraction. You see +B3- in the second line of the control panel. The cell pointer returns to cell B6.

5. **Press the ↑ key twice.**

   Pressing the ↑ key twice moves the cell pointer to cell B4. This is the second cell that you want to include. You see +B3-B4 in the second line of the control panel.

   If you use a mouse, you can point to the cell and click.

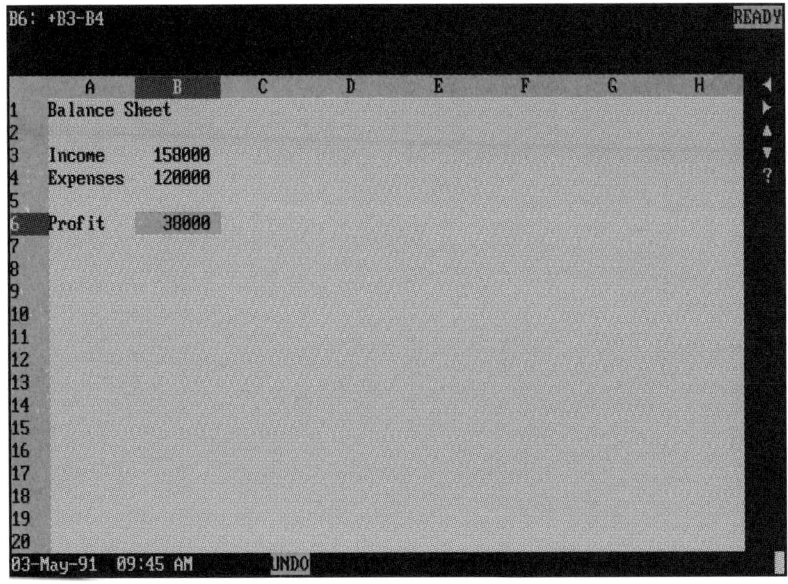

after

6. Press **Enter**.

   Pressing Enter tells 1-2-3 that you are finished with the formula. You see the results of the formula (`38000`) in cell B6. You see the formula `+B3-B4` in the control panel.

   This formula subtracts total expenses from total income.

Why use a formula?
A formula references a cell's contents, not a fixed value. Therefore, when you change the values in cells, the formula's result automatically adjusts and recalculates.

REVIEW

To subtract cells

1. Move the cell pointer to the cell in which you want to enter the subtraction formula.
2. Type +.
3. Type or point to the first value that you want to include.
4. Type –.
5. Type or point to the second value.
6. Continue typing – and pointing to values until you include all the ones that you want.
7. Press **Enter**.

Multiply cells

before

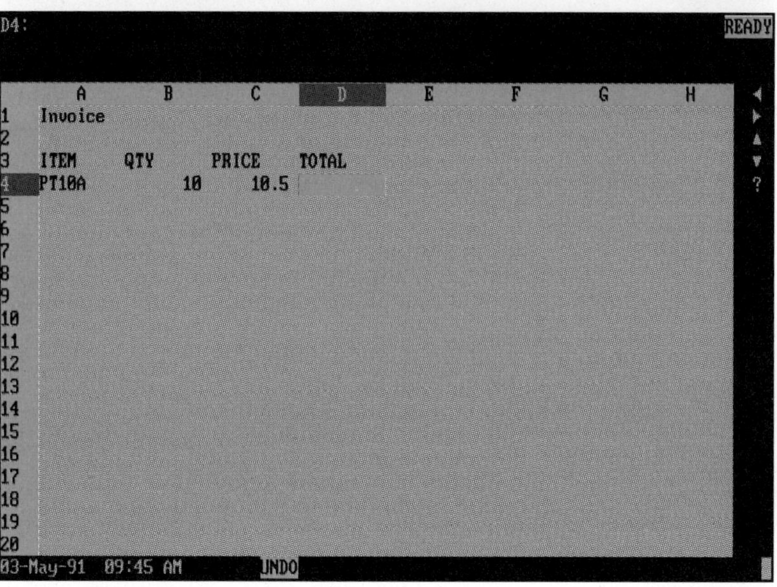

Oops!
To delete the formula, move the cell pointer to the cell and press the Del key.

1. **Use the arrow keys to move the cell pointer to cell D4.**

   You see `D4:` in the control panel and the mode indicator displays `READY`, which tells you that 1-2-3 is ready for an entry.

2. **Type + (plus sign).**

   Typing + places you in `VALUE` mode and tells 1-2-3 that you want to enter a formula.

3. **Press the ← key twice.**

   Pressing the ← key twice moves the cell pointer to cell B4. This is the first cell that you want to include in the formula. You see `+B4` in the second line of the control panel.

   If you use a mouse, you can select the cell by pointing to it and clicking.

4. **Press * (asterisk).**

   The * is the operator. This character tells 1-2-3 which mathematical operation you want to perform. In this case, you are performing multiplication. You see `+B4*` in the second line of the control panel. The cell pointer returns to D4.

5. **Press the ← key once.**

   Pressing the ← key once moves the cell pointer to cell C4. This is the second cell that you want to include. You see `+B4*C4` in the second line of the control panel.

   If you use a mouse, you can select the cell by pointing to it and clicking.

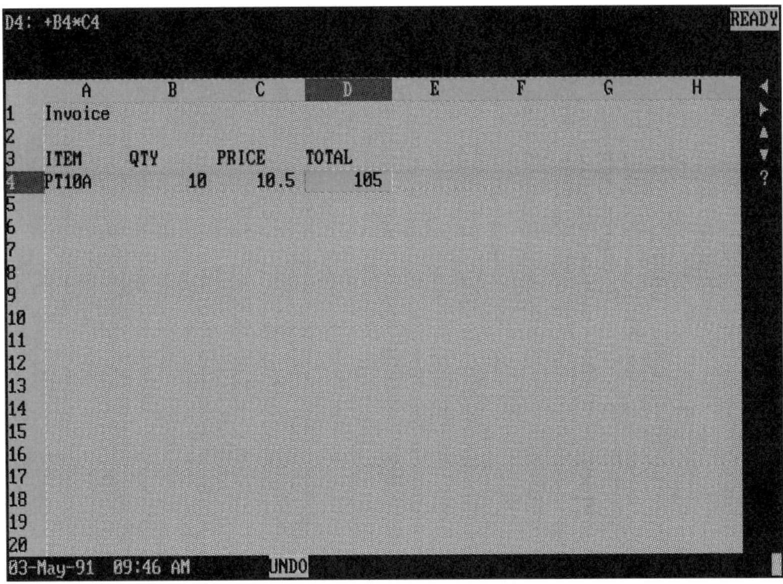

after

Why use a formula?

A formula references a cell's contents, not a fixed value. Therefore, when you change the values in cells, the formula's result automatically adjusts and recalculates.

6. Press **Enter**.

   Pressing Enter tells 1-2-3 that you are finished with the formula. You see the results of the formula (105) in cell D4. You see the formula +B4*C4 in the control panel.

   This formula multiplies the quantity by the price.

REVIEW

To multiply cells

1. Move the cell pointer to the cell in which you want to enter the multiplication formula.
2. Type +.
3. Type or point to the first value that you want to include.
4. Type *.
5. Type or point to the second value that you want to include.
6. Continue typing * and pointing to values until the formula contains all the values that you want.
7. Press **Enter**.

TASK

Divide two cells

before

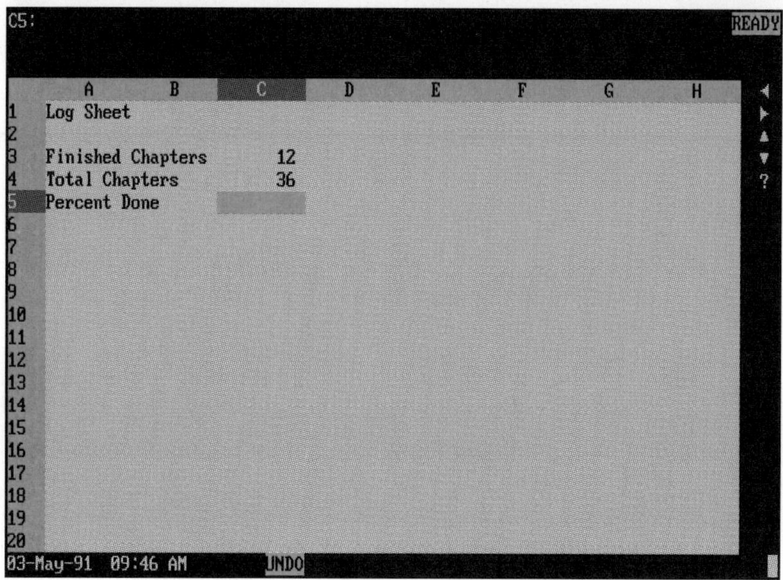

Oops!
To delete the formula, move the cell pointer to the cell and press the Del key.

1. **Use the arrow keys to move the cell pointer to cell C5.**
   You see `C5:` in the control panel. The mode indicator displays `READY`, which tells you that 1-2-3 is ready for an entry.

2. **Type + (plus sign).**
   Typing + places you in `VALUE` mode and tells 1-2-3 that you want to enter a formula.

3. **Press the ↑ key twice.**
   Pressing the ↑ key twice moves the cell pointer to cell C3. This is the first cell that you want to include in the formula. You see `+C3` in the second line of the control panel.

   If you use a mouse, you can select the cell by pointing to it and clicking.

4. **Press / (forward slash).**
   The / is the operator and tells 1-2-3 which mathematical operation you want to perform. In this case, you want to perform division. You see `+C3/` in the second line of the control panel. The cell pointer returns to cell C5.

5. **Press the ↑ key once.**
   Pressing the ↑ key once moves the cell pointer to cell C4. This is the second cell that you want to include. You see `+C3/C4` in the second line of the control panel.

   If you use a mouse, you can select the cell by pointing to it and clicking.

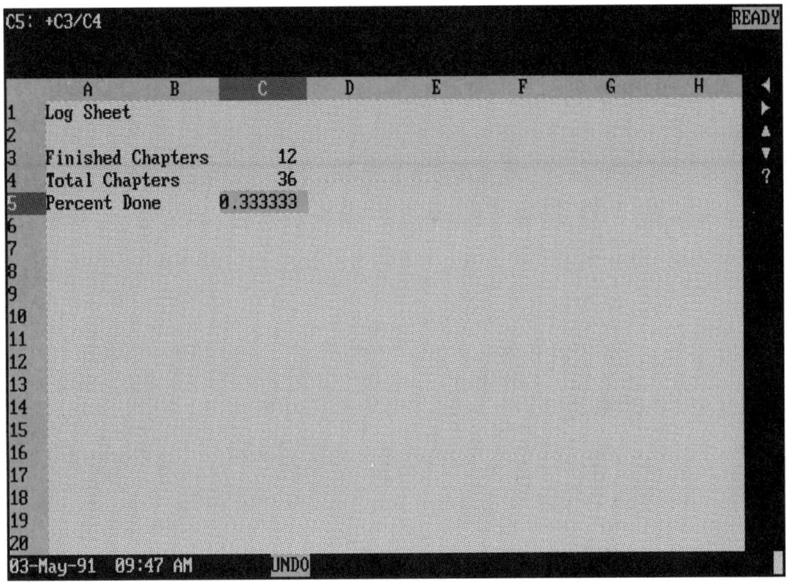

after

6. Press **Enter**.

   Pressing Enter tells 1-2-3 that you are finished with the formula. You see the results of the formula (`0.333333`) in the cell C5. In the control panel, you see the formula `+C3/C4`.

   This formula divides the number of finished chapters by the total number of chapters to calculate the percent finished.

Why use a formula?
A formula references a cell's contents, not a fixed value. Therefore, when you change the values in cells, the formula's result automatically adjusts and recalculates.

REVIEW

To divide two cells

1. Move the cell pointer to the cell in which you want to enter the division formula.
2. Type +.
3. Type or point to the first value that you want to include.
4. Type /.
5. Type or point to the second value that you want to include.
6. Press **Enter**.

Edit a formula
To change a formula rather than deleting it and starting over, see *TASK: Edit a cell.*

TASK

Overwrite a cell

Oops!
To cancel the new entry, press the Esc key before pressing Enter. If you already pressed Enter, press the Alt-F4 key combination immediately after making the change.

before

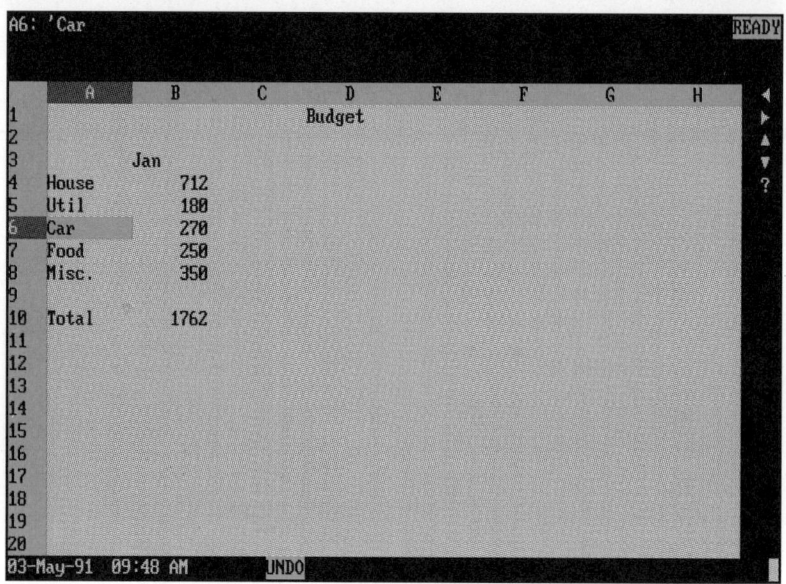

1. Use the arrow keys to move the cell pointer to cell A6.
   You see `A6:` in the control panel, followed by the current entry, `'Car`. The mode indicator displays `READY`, which tells you that 1-2-3 is ready for an entry.
2. Type **Auto**.
   Auto is the new entry. This entry appears in the second line of the control panel; the original entry appears in the first line. The mode indicator displays `LABEL`.
3. Press **Enter**.
   Pressing Enter replaces the previous entry with the new entry.

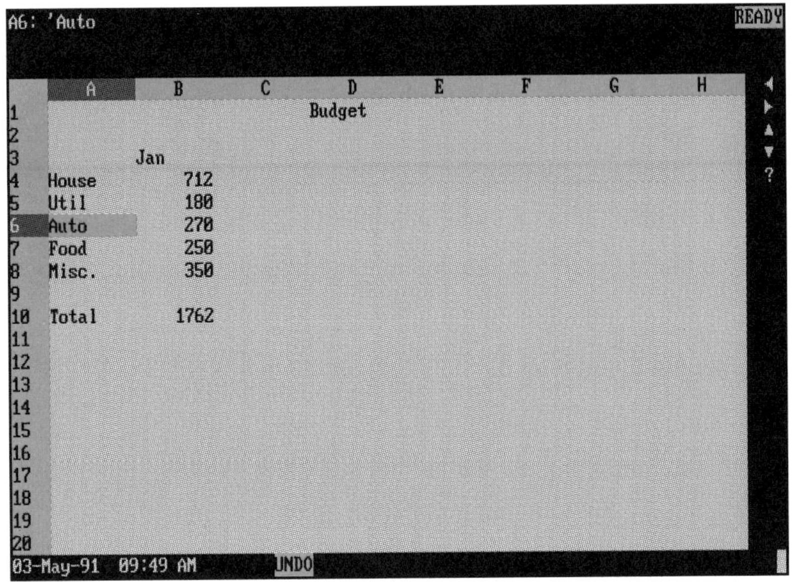

after

Caution!
Be careful not to overwrite formulas. If you type over a formula with a value, you erase (write over) the formula. Therefore, the formula will not be updated.

REVIEW

To overwrite a cell

1. Move the cell pointer to the cell that you want to overwrite.
2. Type the new entry.
3. Press **Enter**.

Know the location of the cell pointer
1-2-3 overwrites the current cell contents if you press Enter, so it's important to know where the cell pointer is at all times.

TASK

Edit a cell

before

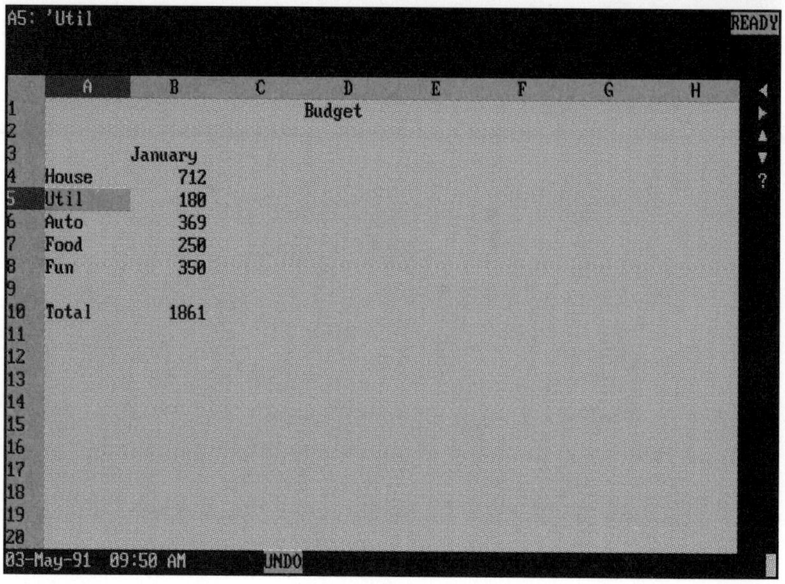

Oops!
To undo the edit, press the Alt-F4 key combination immediately after making a change.

1. **Use the arrow keys to move the cell pointer to cell A5.**
   You see `A5:` in the control panel, followed by the current entry. This cell contains the entry that you want to change. The mode indicator displays `READY`, which tells you that 1-2-3 is ready for an entry.

2. **Press the F2 key.**
   F2 is the Edit key. Pressing the F2 key places you in `EDIT` mode and moves the cursor to the second line in the control panel. The cursor is at the end of the entry.

3. **Type ities.**
   Typing *ities* changes this row label from *Util* to *Utilities*.

4. **Press Enter.**
   Pressing Enter accepts the new entry.

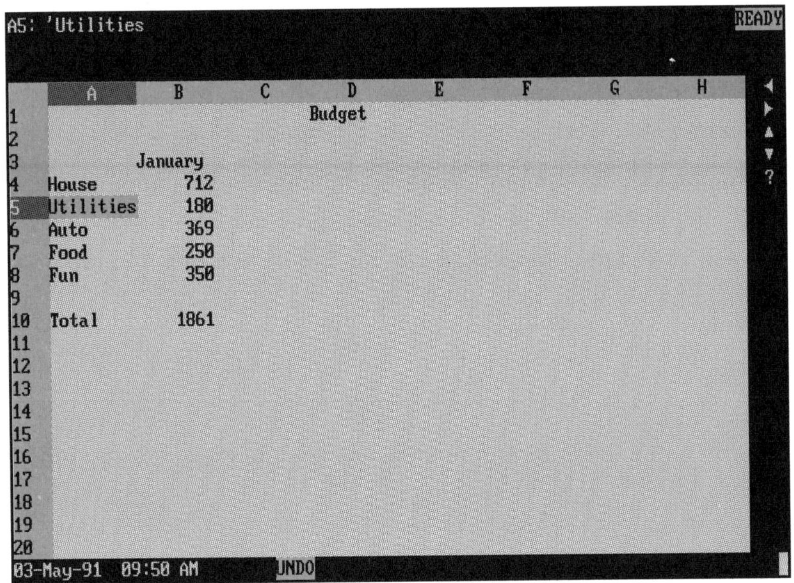

after

Cancel the change
While still in the control panel, you can press the Esc key to cancel the changes.

REVIEW

To edit a cell

1. Move the cell pointer to the cell that you want to edit.
2. Press F2 (Edit).
3. Edit the entry in the control panel.
4. Press Enter.

Overwrite the cell
If the entry is entirely new, overwrite the entry. See *TASK: Overwrite a cell.*

TASK

Erase a cell

before

```
C8: 400                                                      READY

         A         B         C         D         E         F         G         H
1                                   Budget
2
3                  January  February
4   House              712       712
5   Util               180       200
6   Auto               270       300
7   Food               250       325
8   Misc.              350       400
9
10  Total             1762      1937
11
12
13
14
15
16
17
18
19
20
03-May-91  10:00 AM          UNDO
```

Oops!
To undo the deletion, press the Alt-F4 key combination immediately after deleting the cell.

1. **Use the arrow keys to move the cell pointer to cell C8.**

   You see `C8:` in the control panel, followed by the cell entry. This is the cell that you want to erase.

2. **Press Del.**

   Pressing the Del key erases the cell contents. The cell pointer remains in cell C8.

   If the cell that you deleted is included in any formulas, the formulas are recalculated automatically to reflect the change.

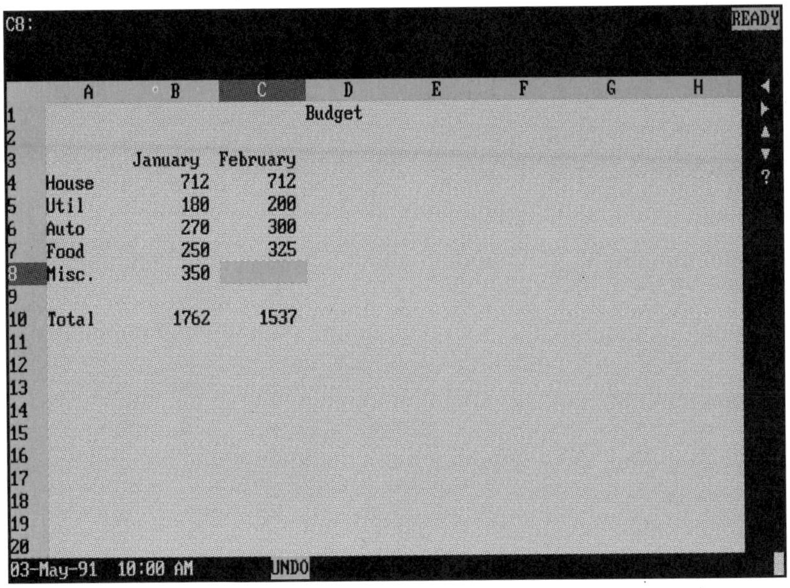

	A	B	C	D	E	F	G	H
1				Budget				
2								
3		January	February					
4	House	712	712					
5	Util	180	200					
6	Auto	270	300					
7	Food	250	325					
8	Misc.	350						
9								
10	Total	1762	1537					

C8: READY

03-May-91 10:00 AM UNDO

after

Delete a range
To delete more than one cell (a range), see *TASK: Erase a range.*

REVIEW

To erase a cell

1. Move the cell pointer to the cell that you want to erase.
2. Press **Del**.

Don't type spaces to erase a cell
Use the Del key to erase a cell; don't type spaces to write over the cell contents. A cell with spaces is not an empty cell.

Copy a cell

before

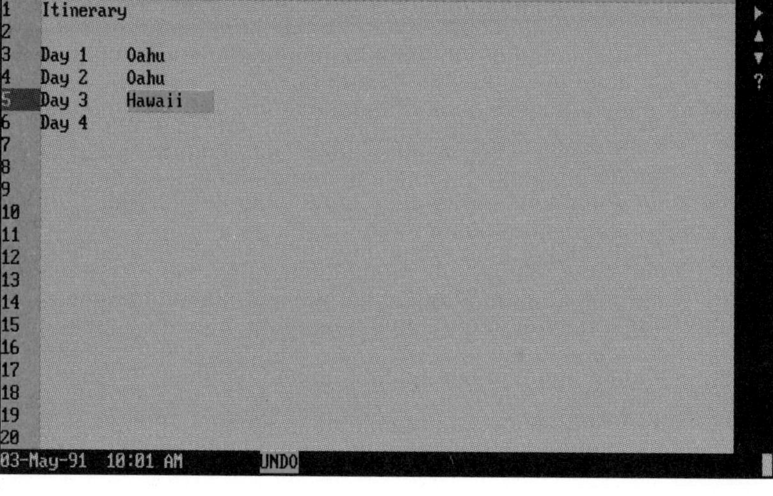

Oops!
To undo the copy, press the Alt-F4 key combination immediately after making the copy.

1. Use the arrow keys to move the cell pointer to cell B5.

   You see `B5:` in the control panel, followed by the cell contents. This is the cell that you want to copy.

2. Type /C.

   Typing /C selects the Copy command. You see the prompt `Copy what? B5..B5` in the second line of the control panel. The mode indicator changes to `POINT` mode. In POINT mode, you can point to the cells that you want to include.

3. Press **Enter**.

   Pressing Enter tells 1-2-3 that you want to copy this cell. If you didn't select the cell in step 1 or if you want to select a different cell, you can type the source cell and press Enter.

   You see the prompt `To where? B5` in the second line of the control panel. B5 is the current cell.

4. Press the ↓ key **once**.

   Pressing the ↓ key once moves the cell pointer to cell B6. This is where you want the copy to appear.

   If you use a mouse, you can select the cell by pointing to it and clicking.

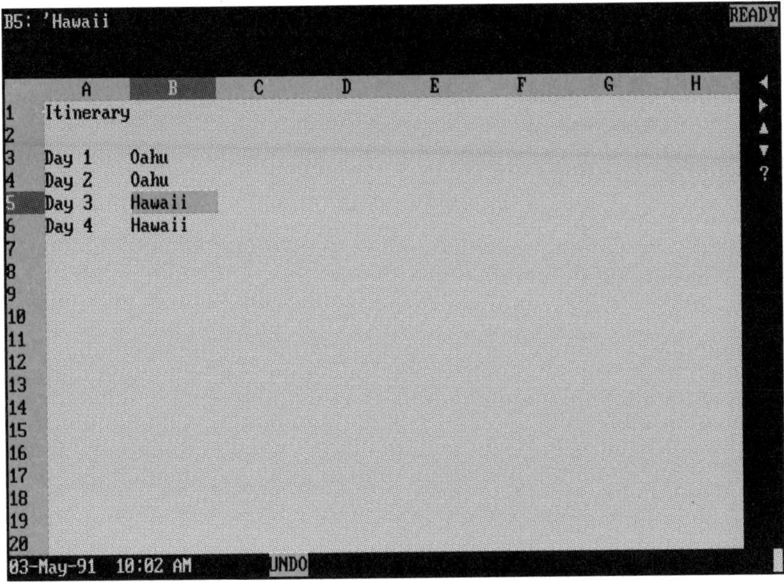

after

5. Press **Enter**.

   Pressing Enter confirms the copy. The entry appears in cell B5 and cell B6. Notice that 1-2-3 copies the entry as well as the format (alignment, protection settings, and so on). See the section *Formatting the Worksheet* for more information on these settings.

   The cell pointer returns to its original location (cell B5).

What is a source cell?
The source cell is the cell that you want to copy or move.

REVIEW

To copy a cell

1. Move the cell pointer to the cell that you want to copy.
2. Type **/C** to select the Copy command.
3. Press **Enter** to accept the current cell or type the address of the source cell.
4. Move the cell pointer to the cell in which you want the copy to appear.
5. Press **Enter**.

Copy formulas and ranges
You also can copy formulas and ranges (more than one cell). See *TASK: Copy a formula* and *TASK: Copy a range.*

TASK

Move a cell

before

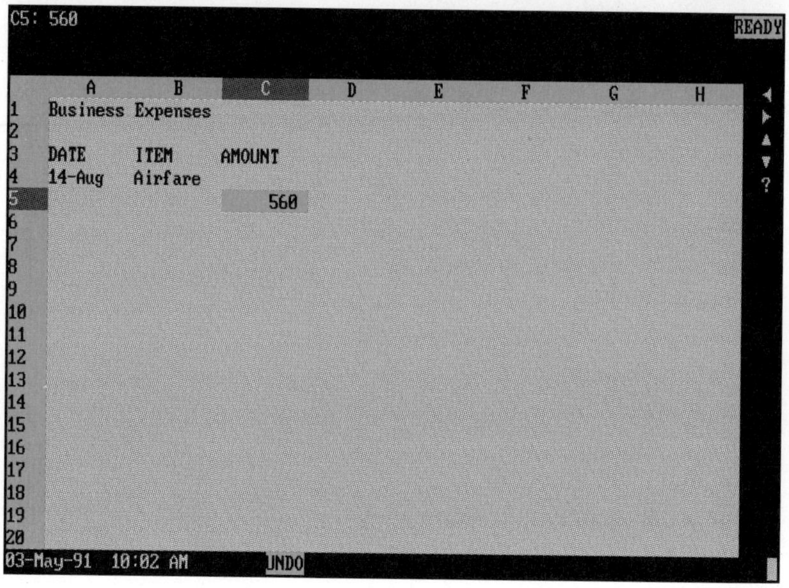

```
C5: 560                                                              READY

     A          B          C          D       E       F       G       H
1    Business Expenses
2
3    DATE       ITEM       AMOUNT
4    14-Aug     Airfare
5                              560
6
7
8
9
10
11
12
13
14
15
16
17
18
19
20
03-May-91  10:02 AM         UNDO
```

Oops!
To undo the move, press the Alt-F4 key combination immediately after making the move.

1. **Use the arrow keys to move the cell pointer to cell C5.**

   You see `C5:` in the control panel, followed by its entry. This is the cell that you want to move. The mode indicator displays `READY`, which tells you that 1-2-3 is ready for an entry.

2. **Type /M.**

   Typing /M selects the Move command. You see the prompt `Move what? C5..C5` in the second line of the control panel. C5 is the current cell. The mode indicator changes to `POINT`. In POINT mode, you can point to the cells that you want to include.

3. **Press Enter.**

   Pressing Enter confirms that you want to move this cell. If you didn't select the cell, or if you want to select a different cell, you can type or point to the source cell.

   You see the prompt `To where? C5` in the second line of the control panel. C5 is the current cell.

4. **Press the ↑ key once.**

   Pressing the ↑ key once moves the cell pointer to cell C4. This cell is the destination, which is the location where you want the entry to appear. (You can type or point to the destination.)

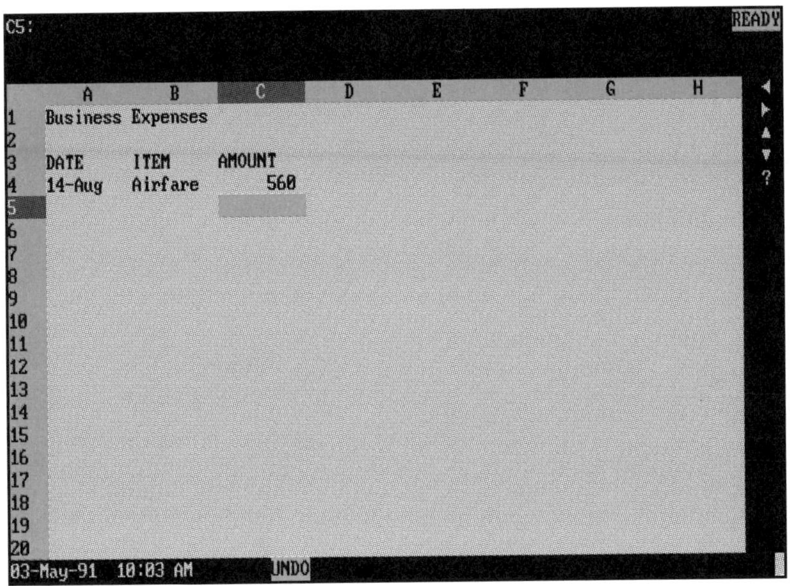

after

5. Press **Enter**.
   Pressing Enter confirms the move. The entry is moved to cell C4, and the original cell (C5) is blank.

What is a source cell?
The source cell is the cell that you want to copy or move.

REVIEW

To move a cell

1. Position the cell pointer in the cell that you want to move.
2. Type **/M** to select the Move command.
3. Press **Enter** to accept the current cell or type the address of the source cell.
4. Move the cell pointer to the cell in which you want the entry to appear.
5. Press **Enter**.

Move a range
To move more than one cell (a range), see *TASK: Move a range.*

TASK

Go to a specific cell

before

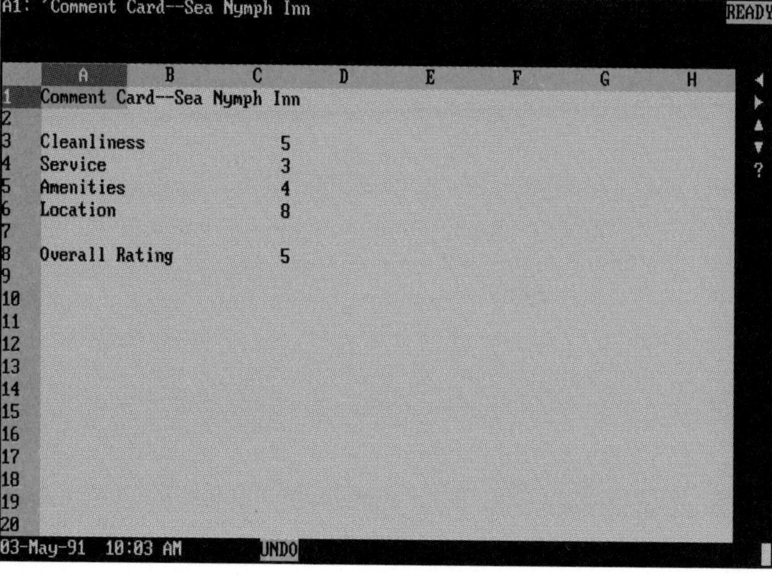

Oops!
To return to the first cell in the worksheet, press the Home key.

1. **Press F5.**

   F5 is the GoTo key. You see the prompt `Enter address to go to: A1` in the control panel. The cell listed is the current cell. The mode indicator displays `POINT`, which tells you that you can use the mouse or arrow keys to point to the cell that you want.

2. **Type C8.**

   C8 is the cell you want to go to. Remember that cells are referenced by the column letter and row number.

3. **Press Enter.**

   When you press Enter, the cell pointer moves to cell C8. The mode indicator changes to `READY`, which tells you that 1-2-3 is ready for an entry.

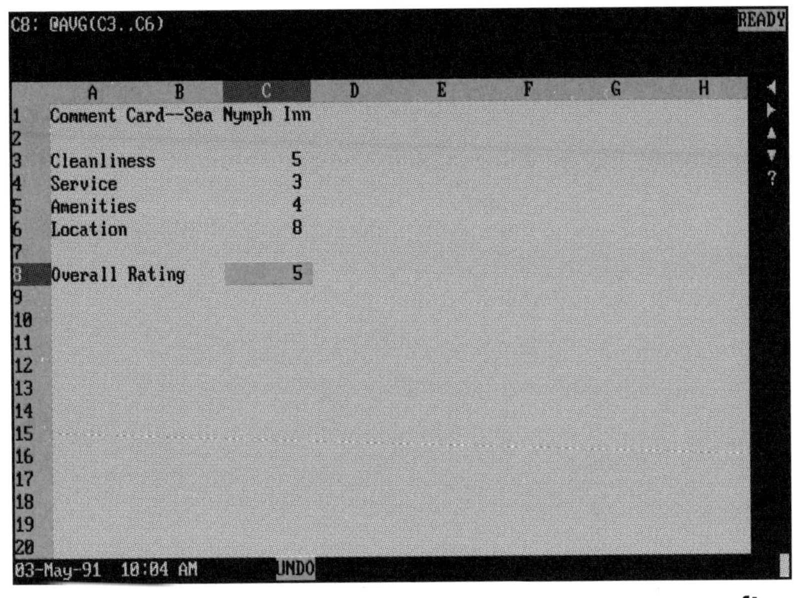

after

REVIEW

To go to a specific cell

1. Press **F5** (GoTo).
2. Type the cell reference.
3. Press **Enter**.

Use Undo

before

```
B10: +B4+B5+B6+B7+B8                                              READY

        A          B          C          D          E          F          G          H
1                                     Budget
2
3                January
4   House              712
5   Utilities          180
6   Car                270
7   Food               250
8   Misc.              450
9
10  Total             1862
11
12
13
14
15
16
17
18
19
20
03-May-91  10:05 AM          UNDO
```

Oops!
Press the Alt-F4 key combination again to undo the undo and retain the changes to a worksheet.

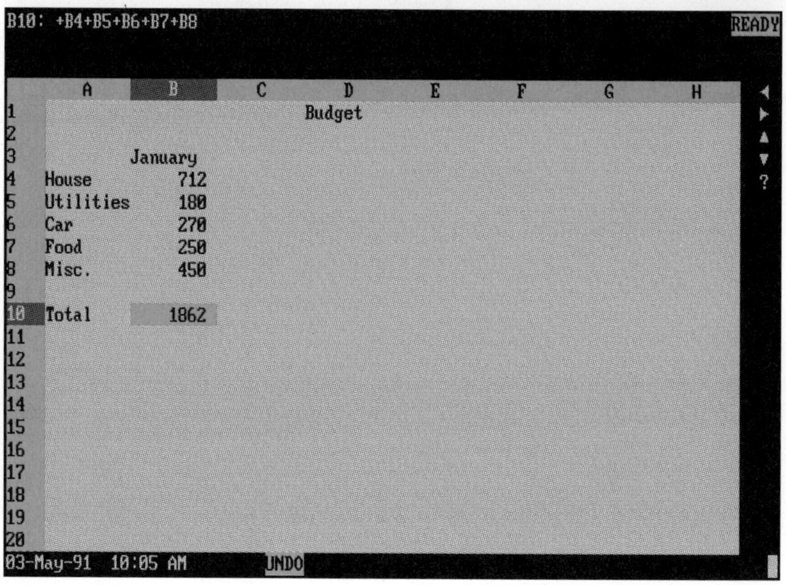

1. **Make sure that Undo has been turned on.**
   For information about turning on Undo, see *TASK: Turn on Undo*.

2. **Use the arrow keys to move the cell pointer to cell B10.**
   You see `B10:` in the control panel, followed by the current entry. The entry is a formula. You will change this formula and then undo the change.

3. **Type 2000.**
   2000 is the new value for cell B10.

4. **Press Enter.**
   Pressing Enter confirms the new entry and overwrites the current entry. This entry, however, is a formula. When you edit the worksheet, you do not want to overwrite formulas. If you do, the results that they calculate may not be correct.

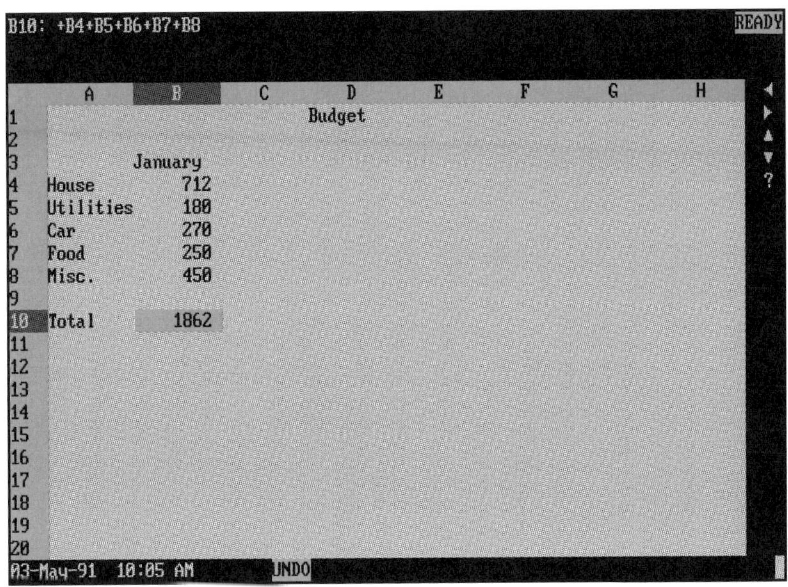

after

5. Press **Alt-F4**.

   Alt-F4 is the Undo key combination. Pressing these keys returns the cell to its original form.

   You must press the Alt-F4 key combination *immediately* after the action that you want to undo. Undo always undoes the last operation that you performed. You cannot undo some changes. Basically, you can undo any changes that you make to worksheet entries, such as deleting entries, moving entries, copying entries, formatting changes, and so on.

Get more information
See your 1-2-3 manual or *Using 1-2-3 for DOS Release 2.3,* Special Edition, for more information about using the Undo command.

REVIEW

To use Undo

Press **Alt-F4** (Undo).

Managing Files

This section covers the following tasks:

Save a worksheet for the first time

Save a worksheet again

Save a worksheet with a new name

Abandon a worksheet

Create a new worksheet

Retrieve a worksheet

Change the directory

Set the default directory

Erase a worksheet file

Save a worksheet for the first time

before

```
 List  ◄  ►  ▲  ▼  ?  ..  A: B: C:                                  FILES
Enter name of file to save: C:\123R23\*.wk1
SAMPMACS.WK1    TUTOR\          WYSIWYG\         WYSYGO\
        A          B          C          D          E          F          G
1                          Sales
2
3                Qtr 1      Qtr 2      Qtr 3      Qtr 4
4  East            800        900       1000       1200
5  West           1450       1235       1678       1980
6  North           700       1000       1544       1890
7  South          1255        890       1345       2000
8
9  Total        $4,205     $4,025     $5,567     $7,070
10
11
12
13
14
15
16
17
18
19
20
03-May-91  10:08 AM
```

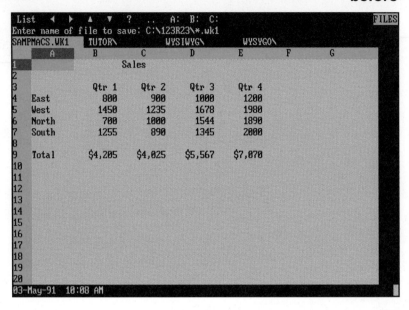

Oops!
1-2-3 prompts you if you type a file name that already exists. Type C to cancel the operation. Then start over, using a different file name.

1. **Type /FS.**

   Typing /FS selects the File Save command. The mode indicator displays `FILES`. The first line of the control panel displays navigation keys; you can use this line with a mouse to move from file name to file name or to move to a different drive or directory.

   The second line of the control panel displays the prompt `Enter name of file to save:`, followed by the current drive, directory name, and `\*.wk1`. WK1 is the extension that 1-2-3 assigns to files. You do not have to erase this extension.

   The third line lists the files in the current directory.

2. **Type SALES.**

   SALES is the file name that you want to assign. You do not have to type an extension. 1-2-3 automatically adds the WK1 extension. The mode indicator displays `EDIT`.

   A file name consists of two parts—the root and the extension. The root can be up to eight characters long. The extension can be up to three characters long and usually indicates the type of file. Separate the root name and extension with a period.

   As a general rule, use only alphanumeric characters for the file name.

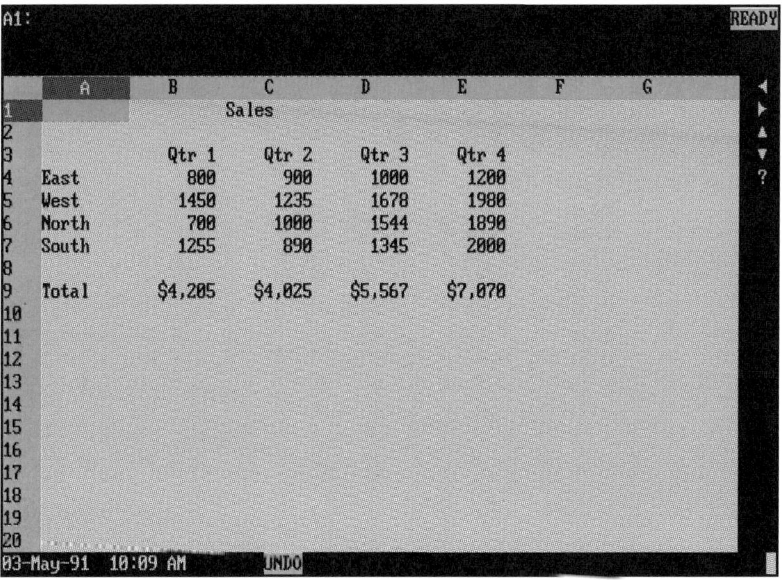

after

Save your data often
Until you save a worksheet, the data is not committed to disk. You can lose data during a power loss.

3. Press **Enter**.

   Pressing Enter saves the file and returns you to the worksheet.

   After you save a worksheet, it is stored on disk. You then can retrieve the data to edit or add more data. As you work on the worksheet, you have only a copy of the worksheet on-screen. The on-screen version and the disk version are different if you make changes. Therefore, you must save the worksheet periodically as you add or edit any data.

REVIEW

To save a worksheet for the first time

1. Type **/FS** to select the File Save command.
2. Type the file name.
3. Press **Enter**.

TASK

Save a worksheet again

before

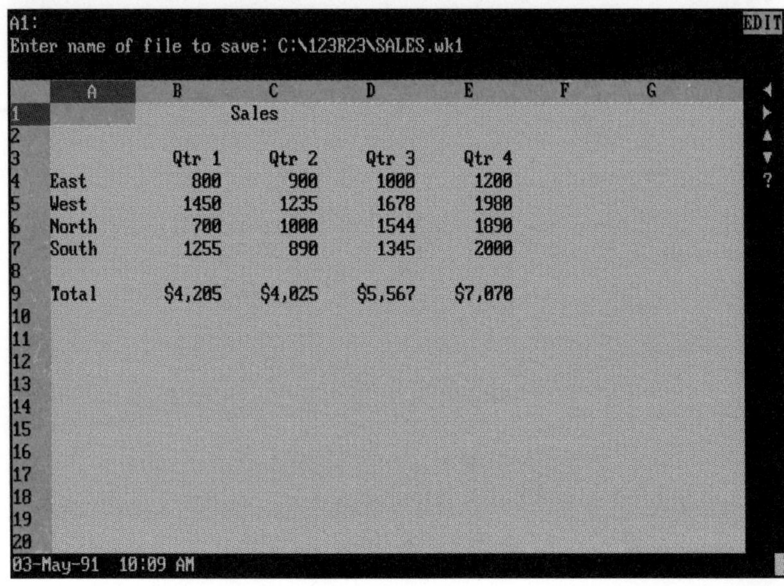

A1:
Enter name of file to save: C:\123R23\SALES.wk1
EDIT
Sales
Qtr 1 Qtr 2 Qtr 3 Qtr 4
East 800 900 1000 1200
West 1450 1235 1678 1980
North 700 1000 1544 1890
South 1255 890 1345 2000
Total $4,205 $4,025 $5,567 $7,070
03-May-91 10:09 AM

Oops!
If you don't want to replace the original version, type C in step 3 to cancel the command.

1. Type **/FS**.

   Typing /FS selects the File Save command. In the second line of the control panel, you see the prompt `Enter name of file to save:`. The current drive, directory, and file name appear after the prompt.

2. Press **Enter**.

   Pressing Enter confirms the file name. In the control panel, you see these choices: Cancel, Replace, and Backup.

3. Type **R**.

   Typing R selects Replace. The mode indicator flashes `WAIT` and then changes to `READY`. The on-screen version of the file is saved to disk, replacing the original version. The worksheet remains on-screen so that you can continue working.

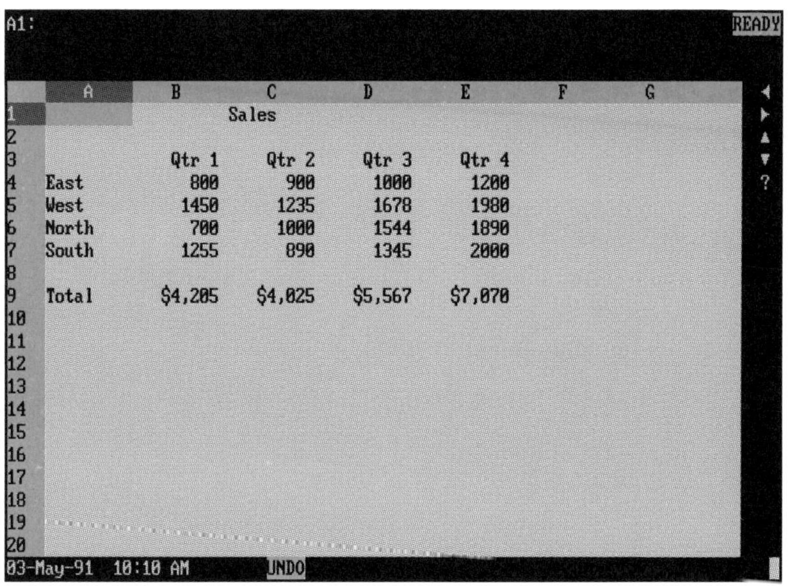

after

Keep both versions of a file
If you want to keep both versions of the file, see *TASK: Save a worksheet with a new name.*

REVIEW

To save a worksheet again

1. Type **/FS** to select the File Save command.
2. Press **Enter**.
3. Type **R** to select Replace.

TASK

Save a worksheet with a new name

before

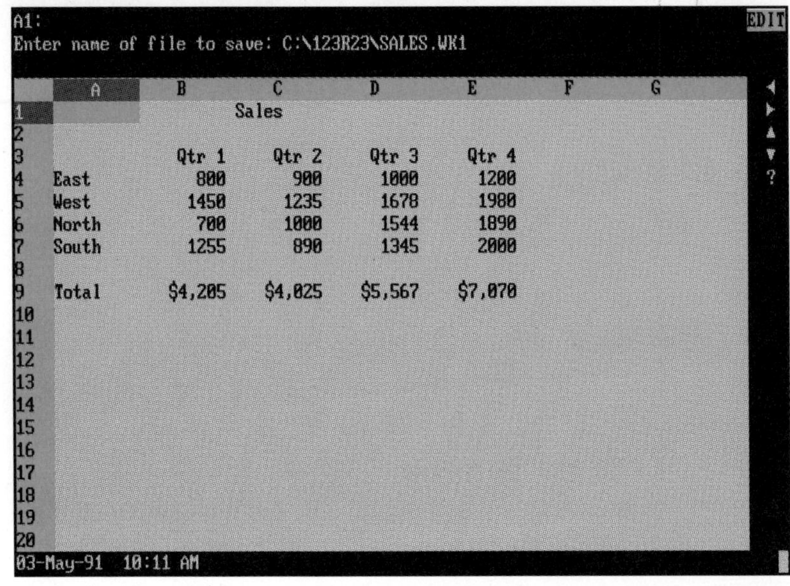

	A	B	C	D	E	F	G
1		Sales					
2							
3		Qtr 1	Qtr 2	Qtr 3	Qtr 4		
4	East	800	900	1000	1200		
5	West	1450	1235	1678	1980		
6	North	700	1000	1544	1890		
7	South	1255	890	1345	2000		
8							
9	Total	$4,205	$4,025	$5,567	$7,070		
10							
11							
12							
13							
14							
15							
16							
17							
18							
19							
20							

Oops!
If you don't want two copies of the same worksheet, delete the copy you do not want. See *TASK: Erase a worksheet file.*

1. Type **/FS**.

   Typing /FS selects the File Save command. You see the prompt `Enter name of file to save:`. The current drive, directory, and file name appear after the prompt.

2. Type **SALE91**.

   SALE91 is the new file name that you want to assign. You do not have to type an extension. 1-2-3 automatically adds the WK1 extension.

3. Press **Enter**.

   Pressing Enter confirms the save and returns you to the worksheet. The new worksheet, SALE91, remains on-screen. The original worksheet remains on disk, intact.

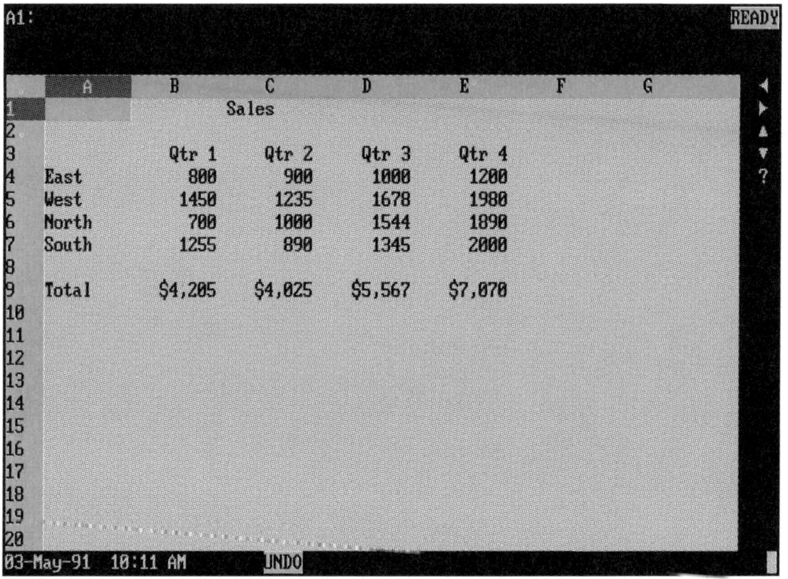

after

Create a template
You can use the File Save command to create a template for similar worksheets. Retrieve the template, make changes, and save it with a different name.

REVIEW

To save a worksheet with a new name

1. Type /FS to select the File Save command.
2. Type the new file name.
3. Press Enter.

TASK

Abandon a worksheet

before

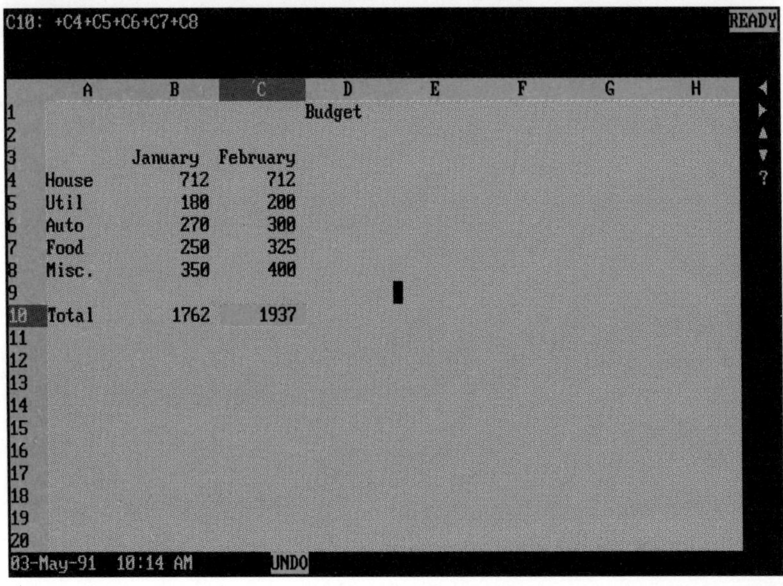

Oops!
If you don't want to abandon the worksheet, type N in step 2. Then save the worksheet.

1. **Type /WE.**

   Typing /WE selects the Worksheet Erase command. You see a prompt that offers two choices: No and Yes.

2. **Type Y.**

   Typing Y confirms that you want to erase the worksheet from the screen. You see the prompt `WORKSHEET CHANGES NOT SAVED! Erase worksheet anyway?`

   If you haven't made any changes to the worksheet, the program skips this step.

3. **Type Y.**

   Typing Y confirms that you do not want to save the changes. The worksheet closes and a new blank worksheet appears on-screen.

   If you have saved the worksheet before, it is not erased from disk; it is erased from memory. You then can retrieve the previously saved version. If you have not saved the worksheet, it is lost; that is, you cannot retrieve it.

after

REVIEW

To abandon a worksheet

1. Type /WE to select the Worksheet Erase command.
2. Type Y to confirm that you want to erase the worksheet.
3. If you have made changes to the worksheet since you last saved, type Y again to confirm that you don't want to save the changes.

Create a new worksheet

before

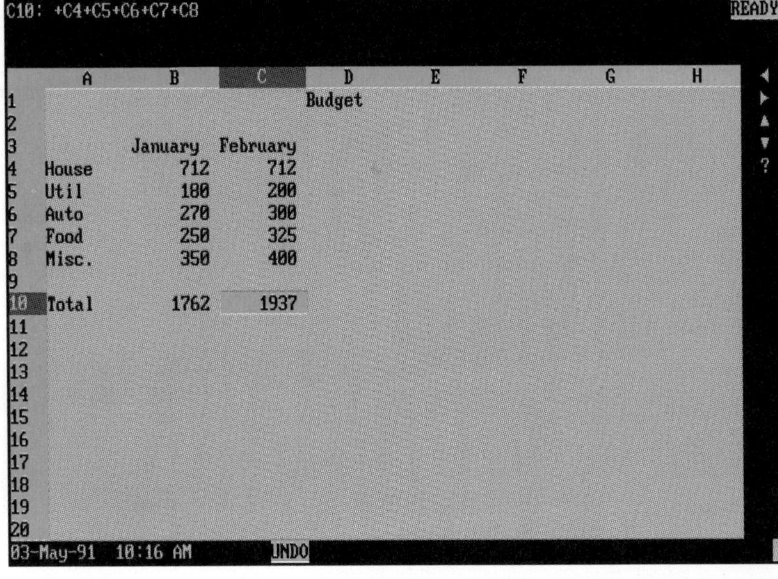

Oops!
If you don't want to close the worksheet, type N in step 3.

1. **Save the current worksheet.**

   To complete this step, see any of the tasks in this section that involve saving the worksheet.

2. **Type /WE.**

   Typing /WE selects the Worksheet Erase command. You see a prompt that offers two choices: No and Yes.

3. **Type Y.**

   Typing Y tells 1-2-3 that you want to erase the worksheet. A new blank worksheet appears on-screen.

   Notice that the worksheet is not erased from disk; it is erased only from memory. You can retrieve the worksheet and work on it again. See *TASK: Retrieve a worksheet*.

   Use this procedure when you want to clear a worksheet and begin working on a new blank worksheet.

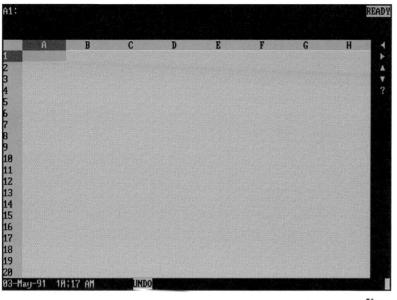

after

Retrieve a worksheet
Use the File Retrieve command to retrieve a closed worksheet. See *TASK: Retrieve a worksheet.*

REVIEW

To create a new worksheet

1. Save the worksheet.
2. Type **/WE** to select the Worksheet Erase command.
3. Type **Y**.

Close unsaved worksheets
If you have not saved the worksheet, you see the prompt telling you so. Type N and save the worksheet before proceeding.

Retrieve a worksheet

before

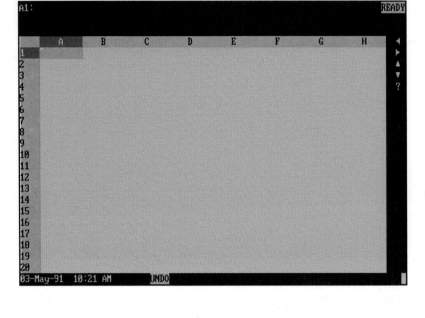

Oops!
If you see a message saying that the file does not exist, you may have typed the wrong name. Press the Esc key and try again.

1. **Save the current worksheet.**

   To complete this step, see any of the tasks on saving a worksheet. You don't have to erase or close the worksheet. When you retrieve a worksheet, 1-2-3 closes the current one. Be sure to save the worksheet so that you don't lose your work.

   If you just started the program and have a blank worksheet on-screen, you don't need to follow this step. Notice that the Before screen shows a blank worksheet.

2. **Type /FR.**

   Typing /FR selects the File Retrieve command. The mode indicator displays `FONT`. On the second line of the control panel, you see the prompt `Name of file to retrieve:`. The current drive, directory, and extension appear after the prompt.

   On the third line, you see a list of file names.

3. **Type SALES.**

   SALES is the name of the file that you want to retrieve.

   You also can select the file that you want to retrieve by using the mouse or arrow keys to point to it in the third line. Only a few file names are listed in the third line, but more may appear to the right or the next line down. Use the arrow keys to scroll to the file name that you want.

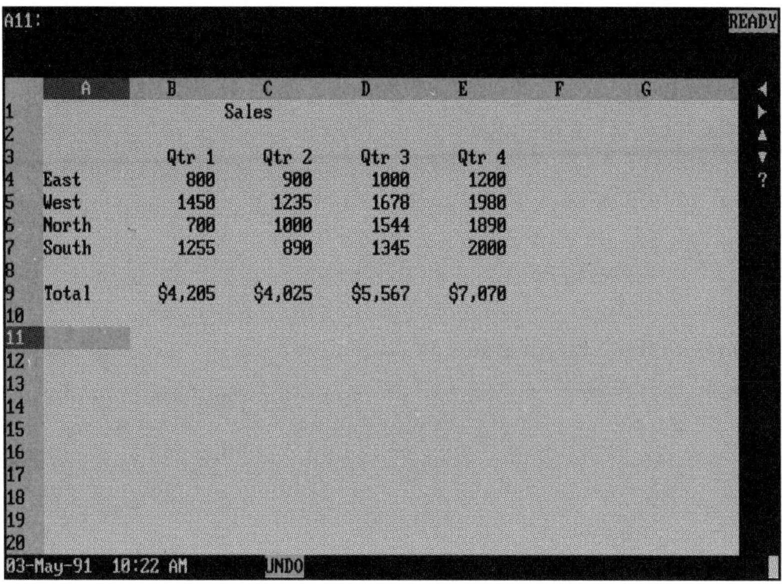

after

See a list of files

To see a full-screen list of files, press the F3 key after typing /FR.

4. Press **Enter**.

   Pressing Enter confirms that you want to retrieve the highlighted file. 1-2-3 closes the current worksheet and retrieves the new one.

   If you do not save the worksheet, you are prompted `WORKSHEET CHANGES NOT SAVED! Retrieve file anyway?` Type **N**, save the file, and start over.

REVIEW

To retrieve a worksheet

1. Type **/FR** to select the File Retrieve command.
2. Type or point to the file name.
3. Press **Enter**.

TASK

Change the directory

before

A11:
Enter current directory: C:\123R23

EDIT

	A	B	C	D	E	F	G
1			Sales				
2							
3		Qtr 1	Qtr 2	Qtr 3	Qtr 4		
4	East	800	900	1000	1200		
5	West	1450	1235	1678	1980		
6	North	700	1000	1544	1890		
7	South	1255	890	1345	2000		
8							
9	Total	$4,205	$4,025	$5,567	$7,070		
10							
11							
12							
13							
14							
15							
16							
17							
18							
19							
20							

03-May-91 10:25 AM

Oops!
If you type a directory that doesn't exist or forget to indicate the drive designation, you receive an error message. Press the Esc key and try again.

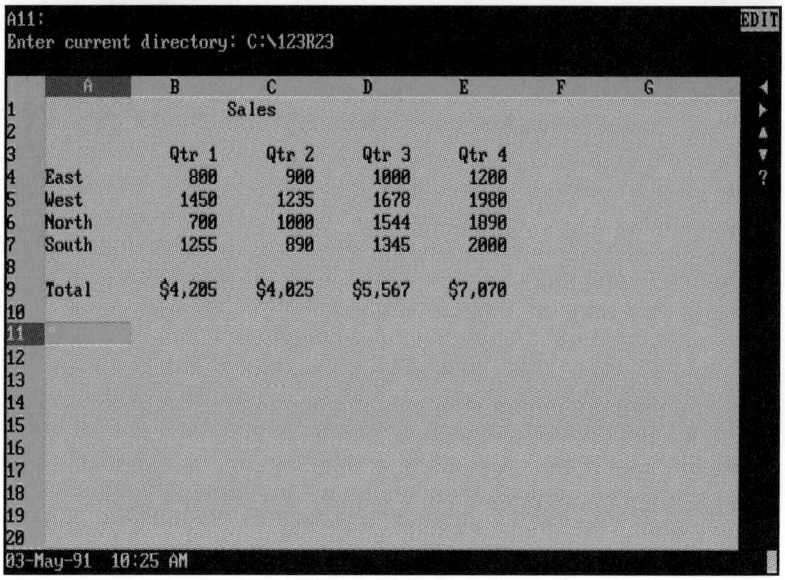

1. **Type /FD.**

   Typing /FD selects the File Directory command. You see the prompt `Enter current directory:`. The current drive and directory appear after the prompt.

2. **Type C:\DATA.**

   DATA is the directory you want to use. You must type the drive letter C:\ before typing the directory name. If your disk does not have a directory named DATA, type one that you do have. Directories are created in DOS.

3. **Press Enter.**

   Pressing Enter confirms the new directory name. Now when you use any of the File commands, 1-2-3 uses this directory. That is, 1-2-3 lists the files in this directory and saves any new files to this directory.

   This directory is in effect for the current work session only. If you quit and restart the program, the default directory is used. To set the default directory, see *TASK: Set the default directory*.

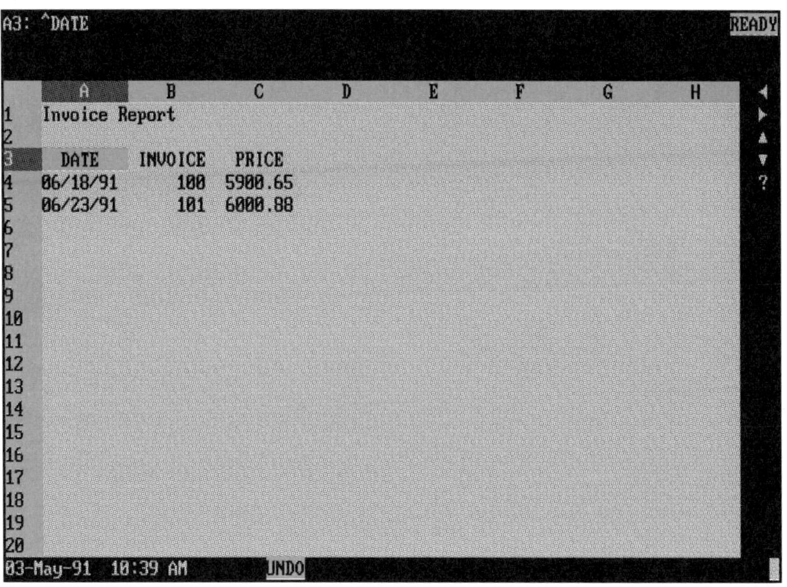

after

Use another directory
If you later want to use a different directory, follow this same procedure to change the directory again.

REVIEW

To change the directory

1. Type /**FD** to select the File Directory command.
2. Type the new directory name, including the drive designation.
3. Press **Enter**.

Create a directory
You can create a directory using the DOS MD (make directory) command. See your DOS manual for more information.

Set the default directory

before

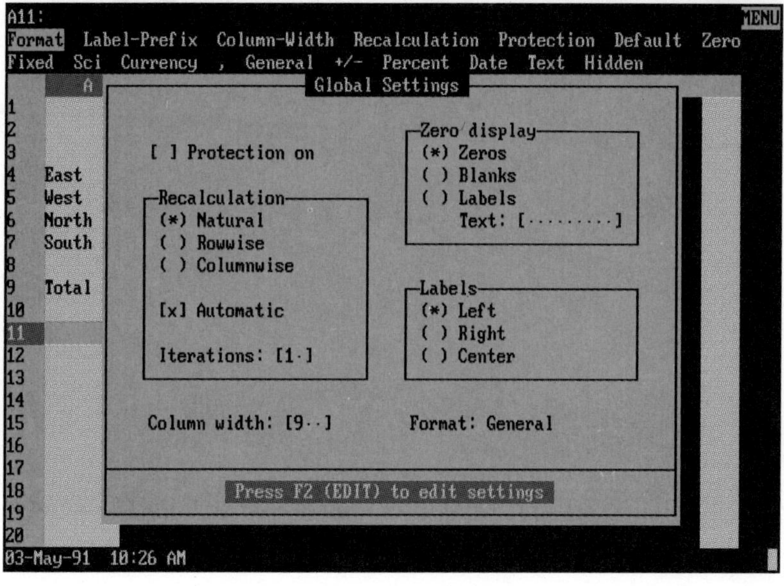

Oops!
If your changes to the default directory are not retained, follow the steps again and make sure that you type U in step 7.

1. **Type /WG.**
   Typing /WG selects the Worksheet Global command. You see the Global Settings dialog box in the middle of the screen.

2. **Type D.**
   Typing D selects Default. You see the Default Settings dialog box in the middle of the screen. The first entry in the dialog box displays the current directory.

3. **Type D.**
   Typing D selects Directory. You see the prompt `Enter default directory:`. The current drive and directory name appear after the prompt.

4. **Press Esc.**
   Pressing the Esc key clears the current directory.

5. **Type C:\DATA.**
   Typing *C:\DATA* sets this directory as the default. You can only specify a directory that you have created already. Directories are created in DOS.

6. **Press Enter.**
   Pressing Enter confirms the new default directory. This directory is listed in the Default Settings dialog box.

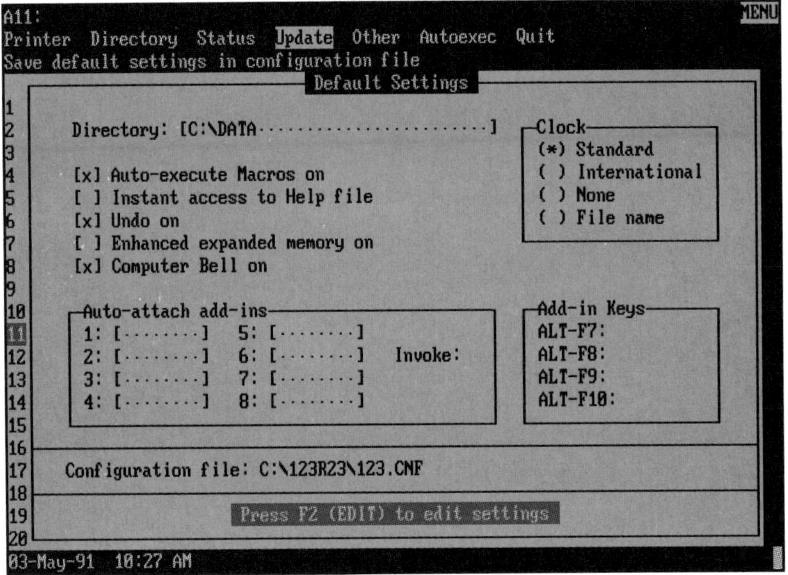

after

Create a directory
You can create a directory using the DOS MD (make directory) command. See your DOS manual for more information.

7. Type **U**.

   Typing U selects Update. The mode indicator flashes WAIT while 1-2-3 updates the settings. You must select this command to update the settings. If you don't type U, the settings are not saved.

   Now when you start the program, 1-2-3 uses this directory to list and save files.

8. Type **Q**.

   Typing Q returns you to the worksheet.

REVIEW

To set the default directory

1. Type **/WGD** to select the Worksheet Global Default command.
2. Type **D** to select Directory.
3. Press **Esc** to clear the current directory name.
4. Type the new directory name.
5. Press **Enter**.
6. Type **U** to select Update.
7. Type **Q** to select Quit.

Erase a worksheet file

before

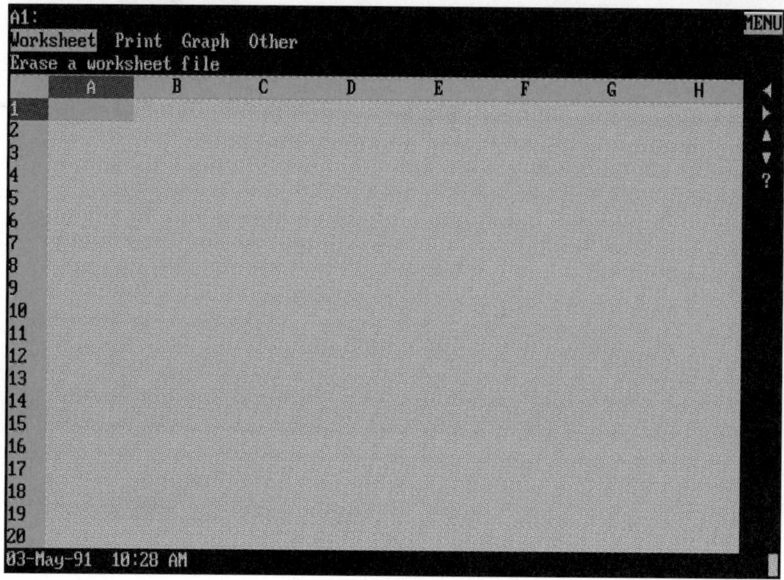

Oops!
If you see a message saying that the file does not exist, you may have typed the file name incorrectly. Press the Esc key and try again.

1. Type **/FE**.

   Typing /FE selects the File Erase command. You see these choices in the control panel: Worksheet, Print, Graph, and Other.

2. Type **W**.

   Typing W tells 1-2-3 what you want to erase. In this case, you are erasing a worksheet. In the second line of the control panel, you see the prompt `Enter name of file to erase:`. A file list appears in the third line of the control panel.

3. Type **SALES**.

   SALES is the worksheet that you want to erase.

   You also can use the mouse or the arrow keys to point to the file name. The file name is listed in the third line of the control panel.

4. Press **Enter**.

   Pressing Enter confirms the name of the file that you want to erase. You see a prompt that offers two choices: No and Yes.

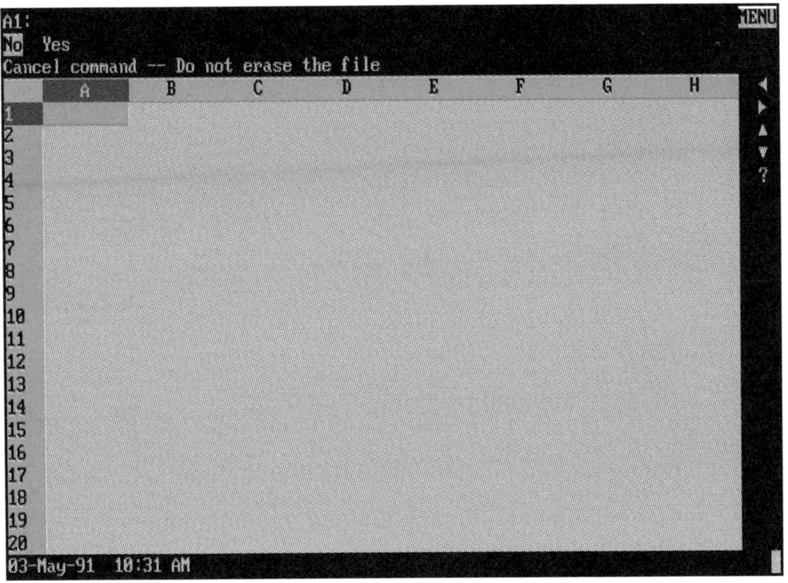

after

Be careful!
Answer N in step 5 if you are not sure that you want to erase the file. You cannot undelete a file without the help of a special utility program.

5. Type **Y**.

   Typing Y confirms the deletion.

   Notice that File Erase erases the file from disk. This command is different from Worksheet Erase, which erases the worksheet from memory.

REVIEW

To erase a worksheet file

1. Type **/FE** to select the File Erase command.
2. Type **W** to select Worksheet.
3. Type or point to the file name that you want to erase.
4. Press **Enter**.
5. Type **Y**.

Should you delete a file?
If you don't know whether you will need a file in the future, do not delete it.

Formatting the Worksheet

This section includes the following tasks:

Set column width

Center a range

Right-justify a range

Display dollar signs

Display commas

Display percentages

Format a date

Format a time

Insert a row

Delete a row

Insert a column

Delete a column

Hide columns

TASK

Set column width

before

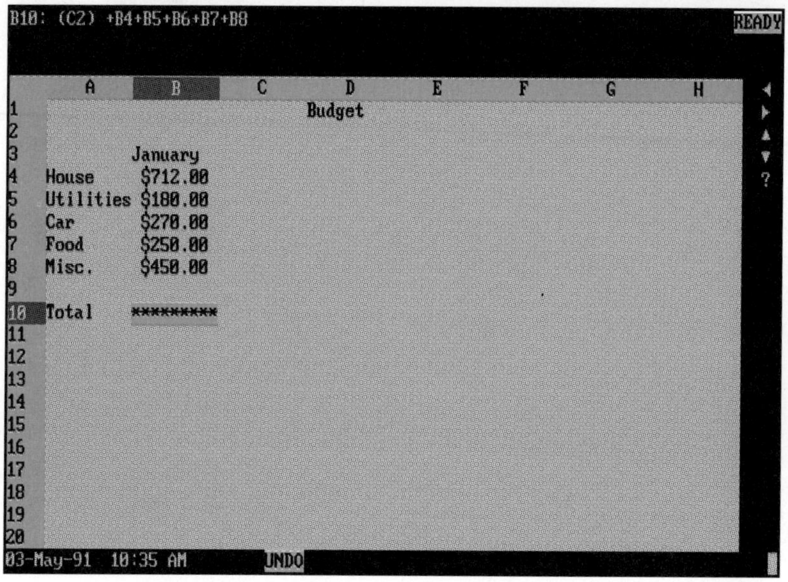

```
B10: (C2) +B4+B5+B6+B7+B8                                    READY

     A          B         C        D        E        F        G        H
1                               Budget
2
3              January
4    House      $712.00
5    Utilities  $180.00
6    Car        $270.00
7    Food       $250.00
8    Misc.      $450.00
9
10   Total      *********
11
12
13
14
15
16
17
18
19
20
03-May-91  10:35 AM       UNDO
```

Oops!
To restore the column's default width, move the cell pointer to the column and type /WCR to select the Worksheet Column Reset-Width command.

1. **Use the arrow keys to move the cell pointer to cell B10.**

   Cell B10 currently displays asterisks. When you see asterisks in a cell, it means that the column is not wide enough to display a value. Formatting often makes the entry larger than the default column width.

   For example, `712` is only three characters long. If you format the number as currency with two decimal places, however, it appears as `$712.00`. This entry takes seven spaces. (For information on formatting, see other tasks in this section.)

   You can position the cell pointer in any cell in the column that you want to change.

2. **Type /WC.**

   Typing /WC selects the Worksheet Column command. You see a list of menu choices.

3. **Type S.**

   Typing S selects the Set-Width command. You see the prompt `Enter column width (1..240): 9`. The default column width is nine. You can enter any number from 1 to 240. The mode indicator changes to `POINT`.

4. **Type 12.**

   Typing 12 sets the column width to 12 spaces.

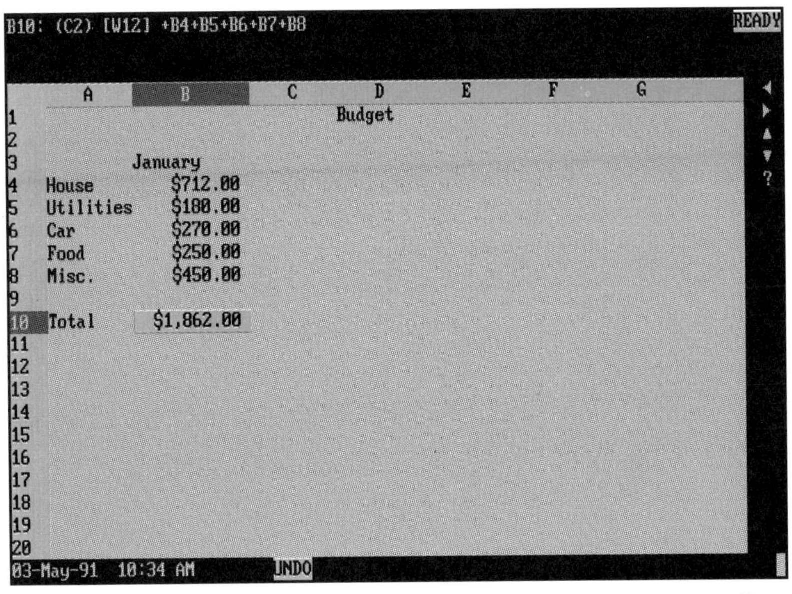

after

How 1-2-3 handles long text entries
If a text entry is too long, you see only part of the entry. You don't see asterisks, as you do with a value entry that is too long.

5. Press **Enter**.

   Pressing Enter confirms the new column width. The column is widened. If some cells in the column still display asterisks, you need to widen the column even more.

   You can tell that the column width has been changed by looking at the control panel. For all entries in this column, you see [W12], which tells you that the width is set at 12. In this example, you also see other formatting codes. These codes are discussed in this section.

REVIEW

To set column width

1. Move the cell pointer to any cell in the column that you want to change.
2. Type **/WCS** to select the Worksheet Column Set-Width command.
3. Type the new width or press the ← or → key to decrease or increase the current column width.
4. Press **Enter**.

Use the arrow keys
You also can use the ← or → key to set the column width visually.

TASK

Center a range

before

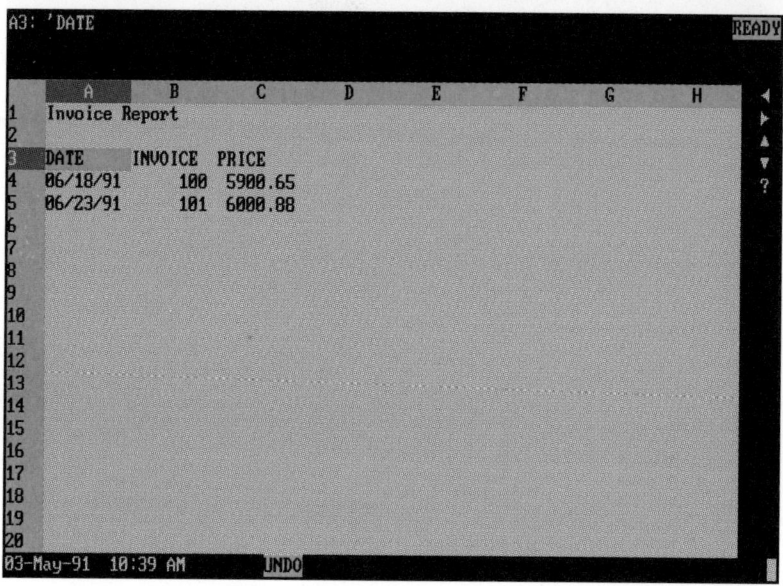

Oops!
To undo the alignment change, press the Alt-F4 key combination immediately after centering the range.

1. **Use the arrow keys to move the cell pointer to cell A3.**

   A3 is the first cell in the range that you want to center. You see `A3:` in the control panel, followed by the current entry. Notice that the entry for this cell is preceded by an apostrophe. This character is the default prefix and indicates a label and left alignment.

2. **Type /RL.**

   Typing /RL selects the Range Label command. You see these choices in the control panel: Left, Right, and Center.

3. **Type C.**

   Typing C selects Center. You see the prompt `Enter range of labels: A3..A3`. A3 is the current cell.

   The mode indicator changes to `POINT`, which reminds you that you can point to the range.

4. **Press the → key twice.**

   Pressing the → key twice highlights the range that you want to center.

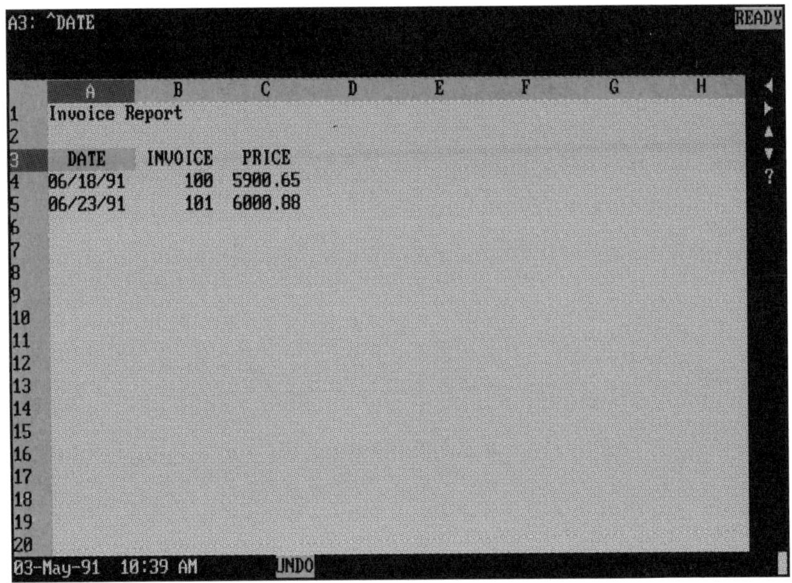

after

What is a range?
A range is any rectangular area of columns and rows. A range can be a cell, a row, a column, or a combination of contiguous columns and rows.

5. Press **Enter**.

   Pressing Enter confirms the range.

   Each entry in the range is centered in its cell. The cell pointer remains in cell A3. Notice that the entry appears as ^DATE in the control panel. The caret (^) is the centering prefix.

   You can type this prefix manually when you enter cells. You also can press the F2 key to move to the beginning of an entry, delete the apostrophe ('), and type ^ to center an entry.

REVIEW

To center a range

1. Move the cell pointer to the first cell in the range you want to change.
2. Type **/RLC** to select the Range Label Center command.
3. Point to the range or type the range address.
4. Press **Enter**.

TASK

Right-justify a range

before

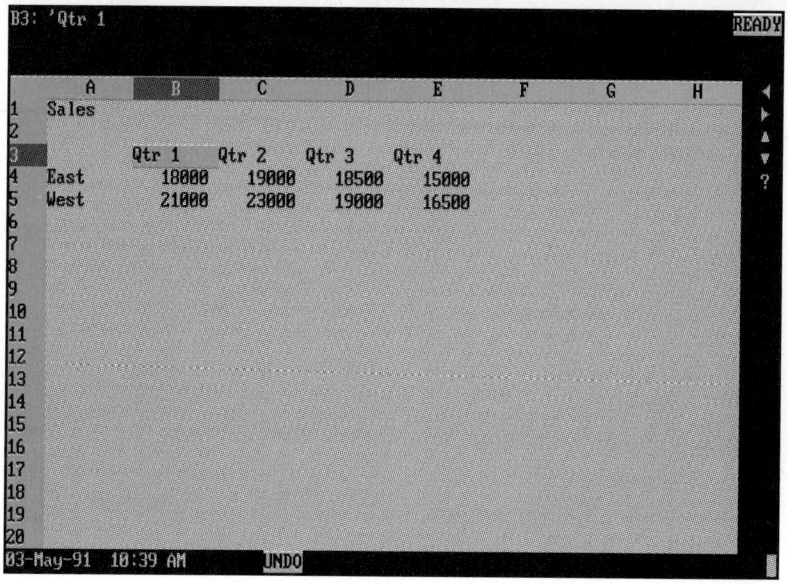

```
B3: 'Qtr 1                                                    READY

        A        B        C        D        E        F        G        H
1   Sales
2
3            Qtr 1    Qtr 2    Qtr 3    Qtr 4
4   East        18000    19000    18500    15000
5   West        21000    23000    19000    16500
6
7
8
9
10
11
12
13
14
15
16
17
18
19
20
03-May-91  10:39 AM       UNDO
```

Oops!
To undo the alignment change, press the Alt-F4 key combination immediately after right-justifying a range.

1. Use the arrow keys to move the cell pointer to cell B3.

   B3 is the first cell in the range that you want to right-justify. You see `B3:` followed by the current entry in the control panel. Notice that the entry for this cell is preceded by an apostrophe. This character is the default prefix and indicates a label and left alignment.

2. Type **/RL**.

   Typing /RL selects the Range Label command. In the control panel, you see these choices: Left, Right, and Center.

3. Type **R**.

   Typing R selects Right. You see the prompt `Enter range of labels B3..B3`. B3 is the current cell. The mode indicator displays `POINT`, which tells you that you can point to the range.

4. Press the → key **three times**.

   Pressing the → key three times selects the range B3..E3. This is the range you want to right-justify.

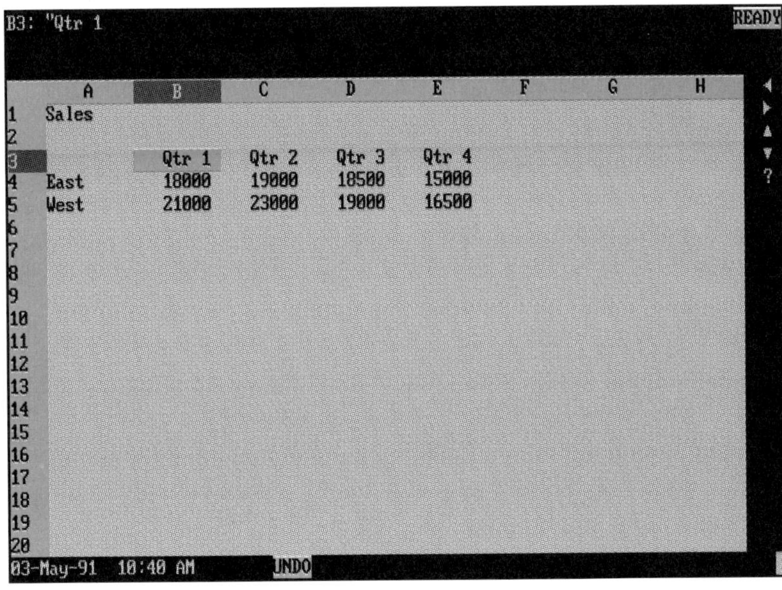

after

5. **Press Enter.**

   Pressing Enter confirms the selected range. The entries in the cells are now right-justified. The cell pointer remains in cell B3. Notice that in the control panel the entry is displayed as `"Qtr 1`. The quotation mark (") is the right-justify prefix.

   You can type this prefix manually when you enter cells. You can also press the F2 key, move to the beginning of an entry, delete the apostrophe, and type " to right-justify an entry.

REVIEW

To right-justify a range

1. Move the cell pointer to the first cell in the range that you want to change.
2. Type **/RLR** to select the Range Label Right command.
3. Point to the range that you want or type the range address.
4. Press **Enter**.

TASK

Display dollar signs

before

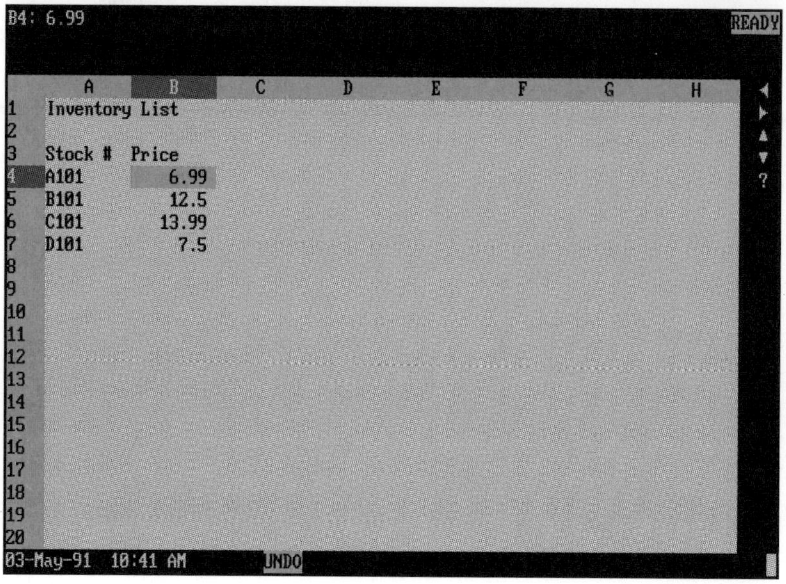

```
B4: 6.99                                                        READY

     A         B        C        D        E        F        G        H
1   Inventory List
2
3   Stock #  Price
4   A101         6.99
5   B101         12.5
6   C101        13.99
7   D101          7.5
8
9
10
11
12
13
14
15
16
17
18
19
20
03-May-91  10:41 AM        UNDO
```

Oops!
To undo the formatting change, press the Alt-F4 key combination immediately after you make the change.

1. **Use the arrow keys to move the cell pointer to cell B4.**
   B4 is the first cell in the range that you want to format.

2. **Type /RF.**
   Typing /RF selects the Range Format command. You see a list of available formats in the control panel.

3. **Type C.**
   Typing C selects Currency from the list of choices. You see the prompt `Enter number of decimal places (0..15): 2`. The default is two. You can enter any number from 0 to 15.

4. **Prcss Enter.**
   Pressing Enter accepts the default of two decimal places. You see the prompt `Enter range to format: B4..B4`. B4 is the current cell. You also see the `POINT` mode indicator, which tells you that you can point to the range.

5. **Press the ↓ key three times.**
   Pressing the ↓ key three times highlights the range B4..B7. This is the range that you want to format.

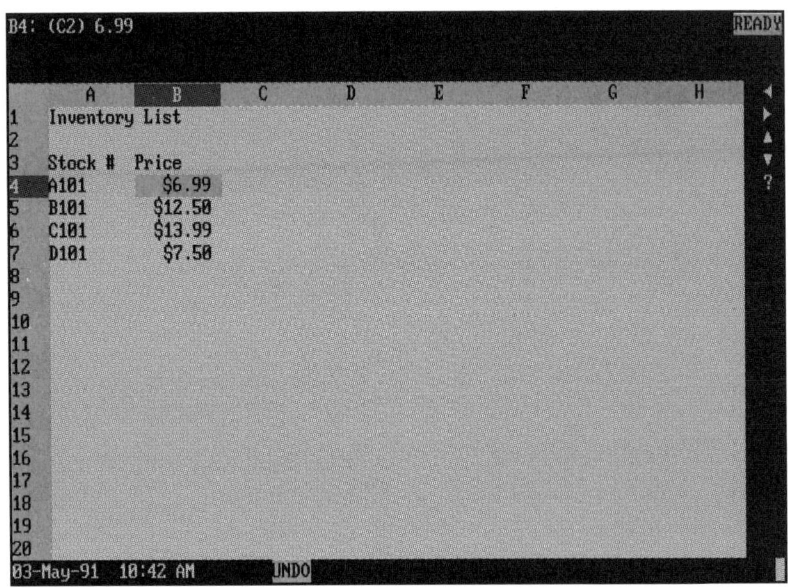

after

Change the column width
If you see asterisks in the column, the entry now is too long to fit in the column. To change the column width, see *TASK: Set column width.*

6. Press **Enter**.

   Pressing Enter confirms the range. The cell pointer remains in cell B4. The control panel displays the entry as you typed it (`6.99`). The contents in the cell, however, are formatted to show dollar signs and two decimal places (`$6.99`).

   The control panel also displays `(C2)` before the entry. This indicates the formatting change (currency with two decimal places).

REVIEW

To display dollar signs

1. Move the cell pointer to the first cell in the range that you want to change.
2. Type **/RFC** to select the Range Format Currency command.
3. Type the number of decimal places.
4. Press **Enter**.
5. Point to the range or type the range address.
6. Press **Enter**.

TASK

Display commas

before

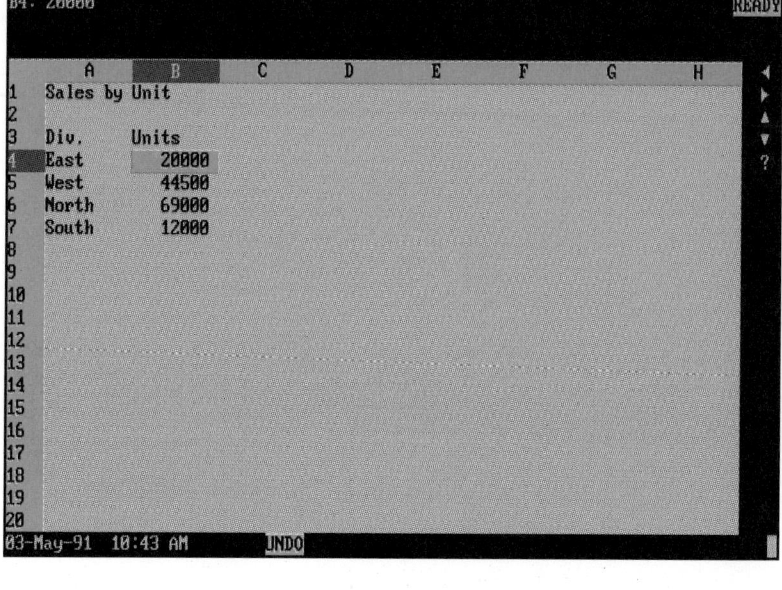

Oops!
To undo the formatting change, press the Alt-F4 key combination immediately after you make the change.

1. Use the arrow keys to move the cell pointer to cell B4.

   B4 is the first cell in the range that you want to format.

2. Type **/RF**.

   Typing /RF selects the Range Format command. You see a list of available formats in the control panel.

3. Type , (comma).

   Typing a comma selects the comma format from the list of choices. You see the prompt `Enter the number of decimal places (0..15): 2`. The default is two. You can enter any number from 0 to 15.

4. Type **0**.

   Typing 0 tells 1-2-3 that you do not want to display any decimal places.

5. Press **Enter**.

   Pressing Enter confirms the decimal places entry. You see the prompt `Enter range to format: B4..B4`. B4 is the current cell. The mode indicator displays `POINT`, which reminds you that you can point to the range.

6. Press the ↓ key **three times**.

   Pressing the ↓ key three times selects the range B4..B7.

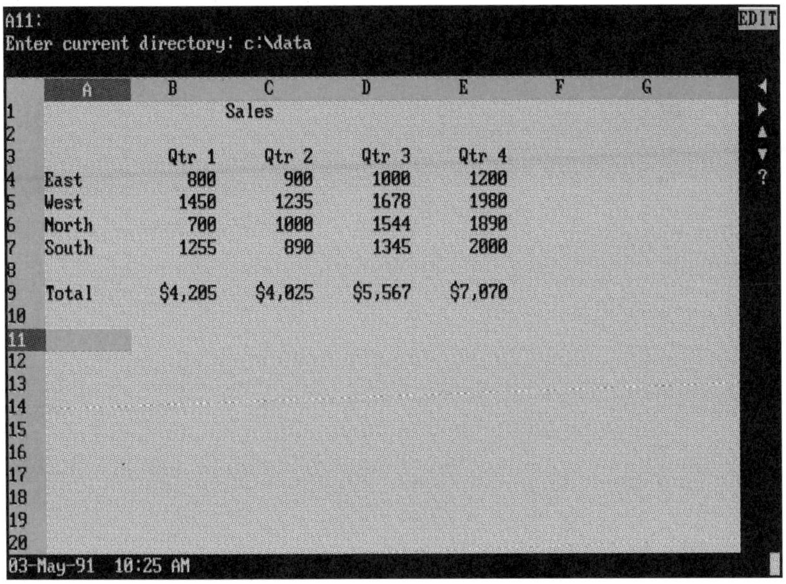

```
A11:                                                          EDIT
Enter current directory: c:\data

       A          B          C          D          E          F          G
1                         Sales
2
3                Qtr 1      Qtr 2      Qtr 3      Qtr 4
4  East            800        900       1000       1200
5  West           1450       1235       1678       1980
6  North           700       1000       1544       1890
7  South          1255        890       1345       2000
8
9  Total        $4,205     $4,025     $5,567     $7,070
10
11
12
13
14
15
16
17
18
19
20
03-May-91  10:25 AM
```

after

7. Press **Enter**.

   Pressing Enter confirms the formatting change. The cell pointer remains in cell B4. The control panel displays the entry as you typed it (`20000`). The contents, however, are formatted to show commas and 0 decimal places (`20,000`).

   The control panel also displays `(,0)` before the entry. This indicates the formatting change (comma with zero decimal places).

Change the column width
If you see asterisks in the column, the entry now is too long to fit in the column. To change the column width, see *TASK: Set column width.*

REVIEW

To display commas

1. Move the cell pointer to the first cell in the range that you want to change.
2. Type **/RF,** (comma) to select the Range Format , (comma) command.
3. Type the desired number of decimal places.
4. Press **Enter**.
5. Point to the range or type the range address.
6. Press **Enter**.

TASK

Display percentages

before

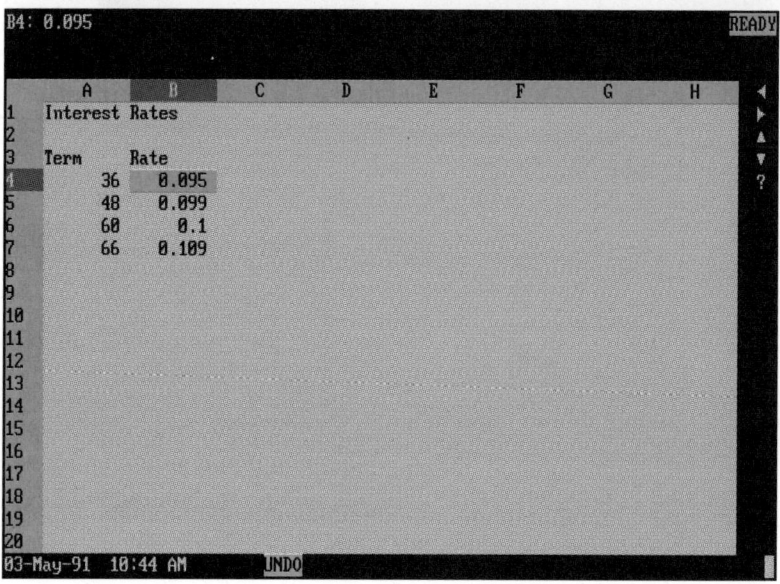

Oops!
To undo the formatting change, press the Alt-F4 key combination immediately after you apply the formatting.

1. **Use the arrow keys to move the cell pointer to cell B4.**
   B4 is the first cell in the range that you want to format.

2. **Type /RF.**
   Typing /RF selects the Range Format command. You see a list of available formats in the control panel.

3. **Type P.**
   Typing P selects the Percent format from the list of choices. You are prompted to enter the number of decimal places. The default is two.

4. **Type 1.**
   Typing 1 tells 1-2-3 to display one decimal place.

5. **Press Enter.**
   Pressing Enter accepts the decimal places entry. You see the prompt `Enter range to format: B4..B4`. B4 is the current cell. You see the `POINT` mode indicator, which tells you that you can point to the range.

6. **Press the ↓ key three times.**
   Pressing the ↓ key three times highlights the range B4..B7. This is the range that you want to change.

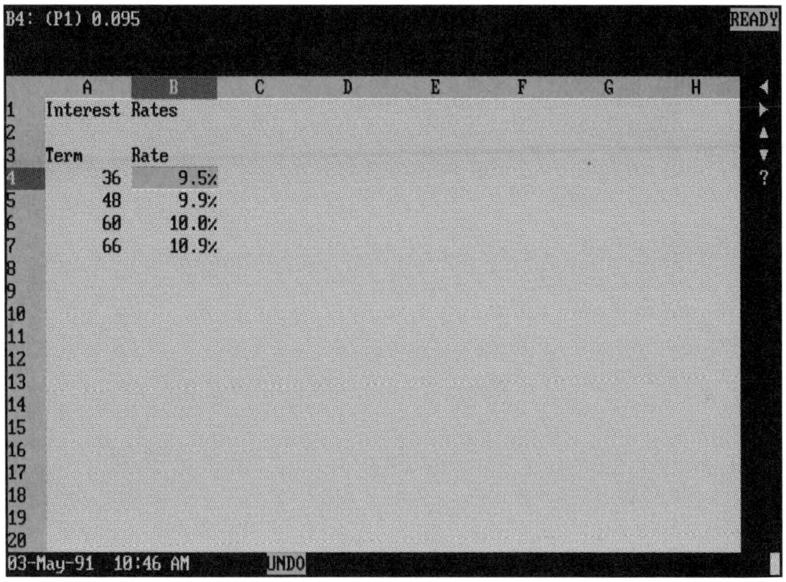

```
B4: (P1) 0.095                                                      READY

          A         B         C         D         E         F         G         H
1   Interest Rates
2
3   Term      Rate
4          36      9.5%
5          48      9.9%
6          60     10.0%
7          66     10.9%
8
9
10
11
12
13
14
15
16
17
18
19
20
03-May-91  10:46 AM        UNDO
```

after

Change the column width
If you see asterisks in the column, the entry is too long to fit in the column. To change the column width, see *TASK: Set column width.*

7. Press **Enter**.

   Pressing Enter confirms the selected range. The cell pointer remains in cell B4. The control panel displays the entry as you typed it (0.095). The contents, however, are formatted to show percent signs and one decimal place (9.5%).

   The control panel also displays (P1) before the entry. This indicates the formatting change (a percentage with one decimal place).

REVIEW

To display percentages

1. Move the cell pointer to the first cell in the range that you want to change.
2. Type **/RFP** to select the Range Format Percent command.
3. Type the number of decimal places.
4. Press **Enter**.
5. Point to the range or type the range address.
6. Press **Enter**.

Enter percents
Notice that all the values are fractions of one. You use this method to enter percents. For example, .1 means 10 percent.

TASK

Format a date

before

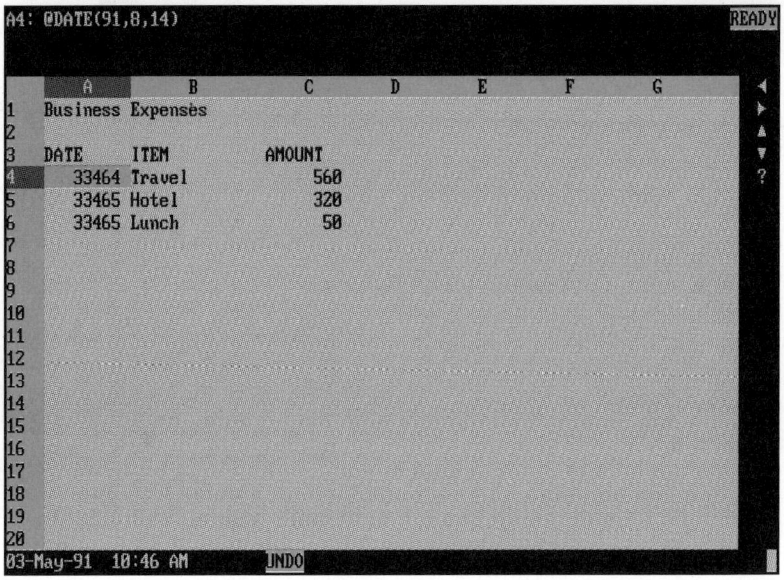

```
A4: @DATE(91,8,14)                                              READY

       A         B          C        D        E        F        G
1   Business Expenses
2
3   DATE     ITEM          AMOUNT
4      33464 Travel           560
5      33465 Hotel            320
6      33465 Lunch             50
7
8
9
10
11
12
13
14
15
16
17
18
19
20
03-May-91  10:46 AM        UNDO
```

Oops!
To undo the formatting change, press the Alt-F4 key combination immediately after you specify the formatting.

1. **Use the arrow keys to move the cell pointer to cell A4.**

   A4 is the first cell in the range that you want to change. In this column, you see date serial numbers.

   Remember that 1-2-3 stores dates in a special way—as serial numbers. To enter dates, you must use a special date function. See *TASK: Enter a date* for more information.

   To display the serial numbers as dates, you must format them.

2. **Type /RF.**

   Typing /RF selects the Range Format command. You see a list of available formats in the control panel.

3. **Type D.**

   Typing D selects Date. You see a list of the date formats.

4. **Type 4.**

   Typing 4 selects the long international date format. This format displays dates as `08/14/91`. (You can change the default international format. See the 1-2-3 manual or *Using 1-2-3 for DOS Release 2.3,* Special Edition, for more information.)

   You see the prompt `Enter range to format: A4..A4`. A4 is the current cell. The mode indicator displays `POINT`, which tells you that you can point to the range.

5. **Press the ↓ key twice.**

   Pressing the ↓ key twice highlights the range A4..A6. This is the range that you want to change.

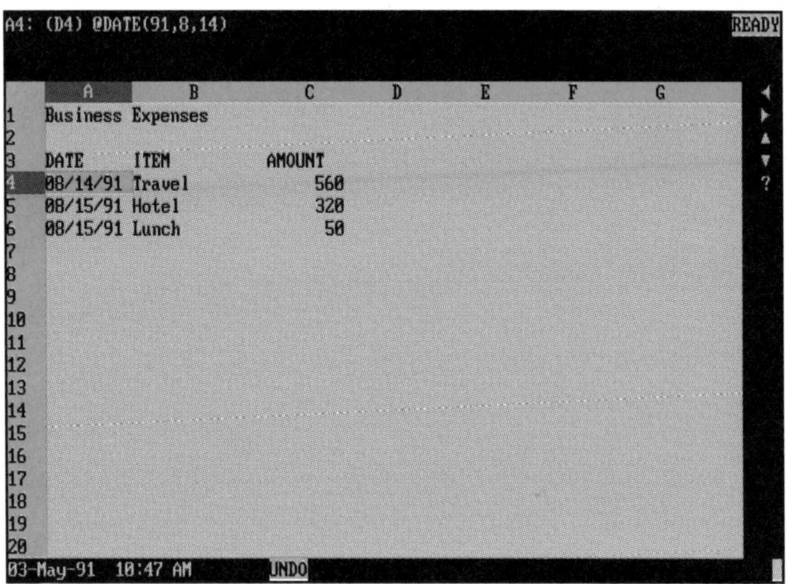

after

6. Press **Enter**.

   The cell displays the date in the format `08/14/91`. You also see the notation `(D4)` in the control panel. This indicates the format change (date in number 4, or long international, format).

Change the column width
If you see asterisks in the column, the entry is too long to fit in the column. To change the column width, see *TASK: Set column width.*

REVIEW

To format a date

1. Move the cell pointer to the first cell in the range you want to change.
2. Type **/RFD** to select the Range Format Date command.
3. Select the date format you want from the following choices:

Number	*Style*	*Example*
1	DD-MMM-YY	14-Aug-91
2	DD-MMM	14-Aug (current year)
3	MMM-YY	Aug-91
4	MM/DD/YY	08/14/91 (long international)
5	MM/DD	08/14 (short international, current year)

4. Type or point to the range that you want.
5. Press **Enter**.

Format a time

before

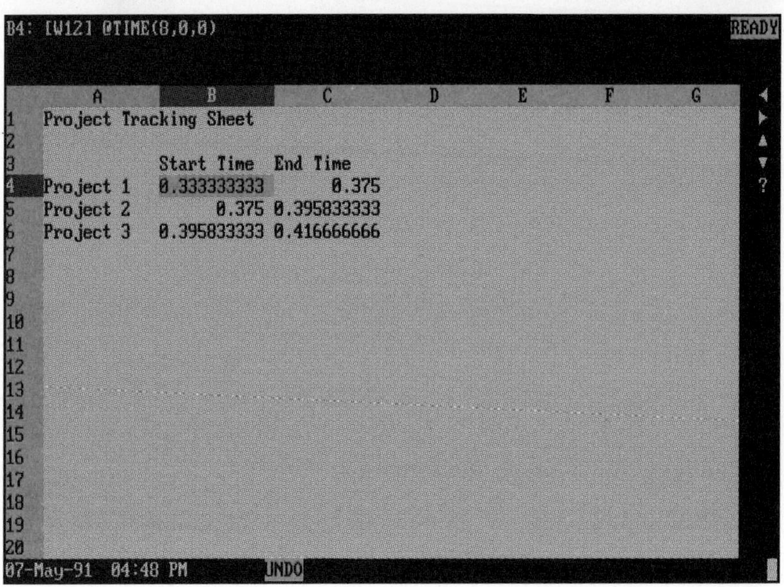

Oops!
To undo the formatting change, press the Alt-F4 key combination immediately after you specify the formatting.

1. **Use the arrow keys to move the cell pointer to cell B4.**
   B4 is the first cell in the range that you want to change. In this cell, you see fractions. Remember that 1-2-3 stores times in a special way—as fractions. To enter a time, you must use a special time function. See *TASK: Enter a time* for more information.

2. **Type /RF.**
   Typing /RF selects the Range Format command. You see a list of available formats in the control panel.

3. **Type D.**
   Typing D selects Date. You see the list of date formats.

4. **Type T.**
   Typing T selects Time. You see the list of time formats.

5. **Type 2.**
   Typing 2 selects the second time format—HH:MM AM/PM.

   You see the prompt `Enter range to format: B4..B4`. B4 is the current cell. The mode indicator displays `POINT`, which reminds you that you can point to the range.

6. **Press the → key once and the ↓ key twice.**
   Pressing these arrow keys highlights the range B4..C6. This is the range that you want to format.

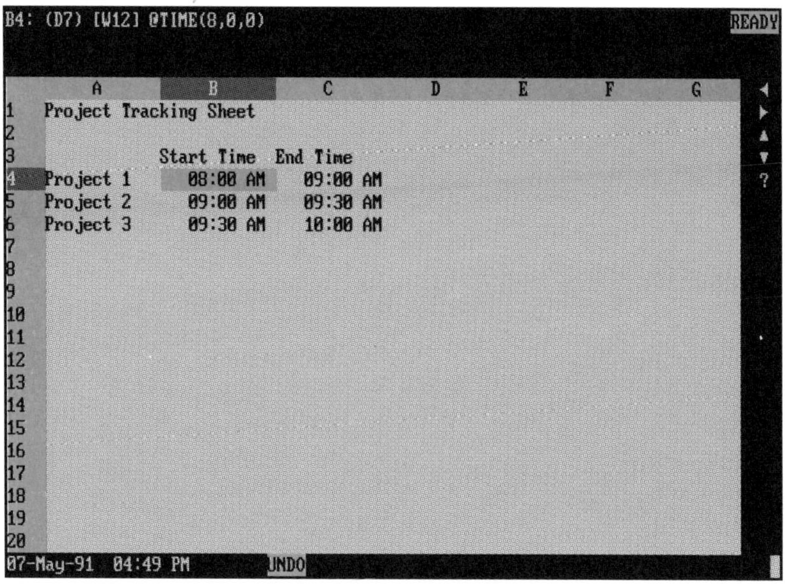

after

Change the column width
If you see asterisks in the column, the entry is too long to fit in the column. To change the column width, see *TASK: Set column width.*

7. Press **Enter**.

   Pressing Enter confirms the selected range. The cell displays the time in the format `08:00 AM`. You also see the notation `(D7)` displayed in the control panel, which indicates the format change.

REVIEW

To format a time

1. Move the cell pointer to the first cell in the range that you want to change.
2. Type **/RFDT** to select the Range Format Date Time command.
3. Select the time format you want from the following choices:

Number	*Style*	*Example*
1	HH:MM:SS AM/PM	11:29:34 AM
2	HH:MM AM/PM	11:29 AM
3	HH:MM:SS	14:00:34 (long int'l, 24-hour clock)
4	HH:MM	14:00 (short int'l, 24-hour clock)

4. Type or point to the range that you want.
5. Press **Enter**.

TASK

Insert a row

before

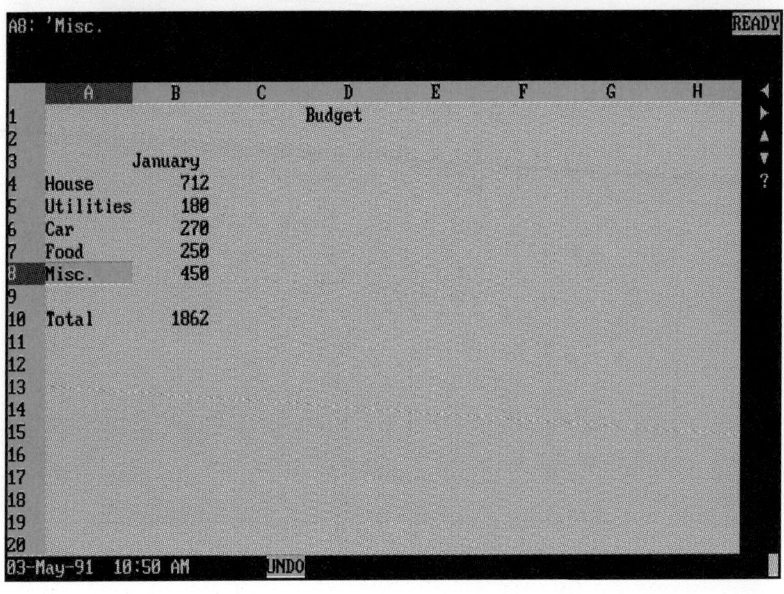

Oops!
To delete the new row, press the Alt-F4 key combination immediately after adding the row.

1. **Use the arrow keys to move the cell pointer to cell A8.**
   You will insert the new row above row 8. You can position the cell pointer in any column in the row.

2. **Type /WI.**
   Typing /WI selects the Worksheet Insert command and displays two choices: Column and Row.

3. **Type R.**
   Typing R selects Row. You see the prompt `Enter row insert range: A8..A8`. A8 is the current cell. The mode indicator changes to `POINT`, which reminds you that you can point at the range.

4. **Press Enter.**
   Pressing Enter inserts one blank row.

   You can also insert more than one row. Simply type the range address for the number of rows that you want to insert. For example, type *A8..A10* to insert three rows. The cell pointer remains in the first cell of the range.

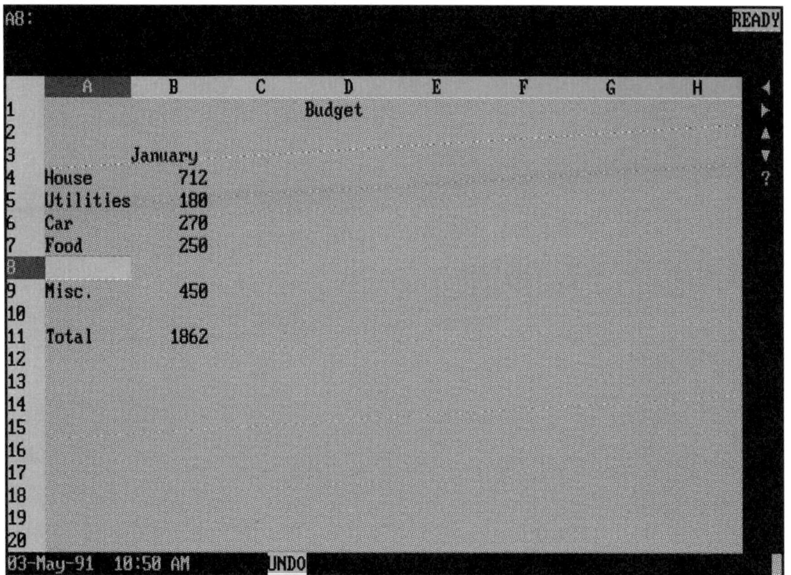

after

Formatting the new row
Any special cell formats that are already in the worksheet are not copied to the new row automatically. You have to format all the columns in the row.

REVIEW

To insert a row

1. Move the cell pointer to where you want to insert the row.
2. Type **/WIR** to select the Worksheet Insert Row command.
3. Type the range address of the row(s) that you want to insert.
4. Press **Enter**.

TASK

Delete a row

before

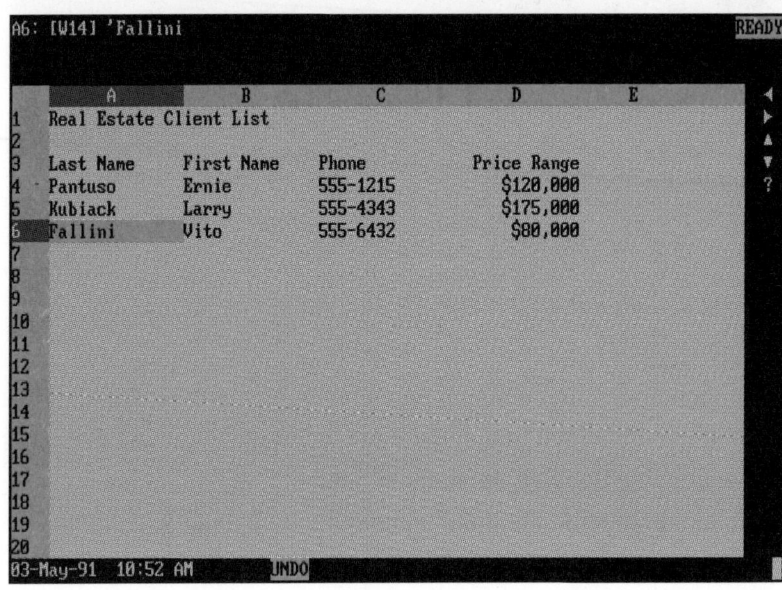

A6: [W14] 'Fallini
READY
A B C D E
1 Real Estate Client List
3 Last Name First Name Phone Price Range
4 Pantuso Ernie 555-1215 $120,000
5 Kubiack Larry 555-4343 $175,000
6 Fallini Vito 555-6432 $80,000
03-May-91 10:52 AM UNDO

Oops!
To restore a row, press the Alt-F4 key combination immediately after deleting the row.

1. **Use the arrow keys to move the cell pointer to cell A6.**
   Row 6 is the row that you want to delete. You can place the cell pointer in any column in the row.

2. **Type /WD.**
   Typing /WD selects the Worksheet Delete command and displays two choices: Column and Row.

3. **Type R.**
   Typing R selects Row. You see the prompt `Enter range of rows to delete: A6..A6`. A6 is the current cell.

4. **Press Enter.**
   Pressing Enter deletes the current row. You can delete more than one row. Simply type the range address of the rows that you want to delete. For example, type *A6..A8* to delete three rows.

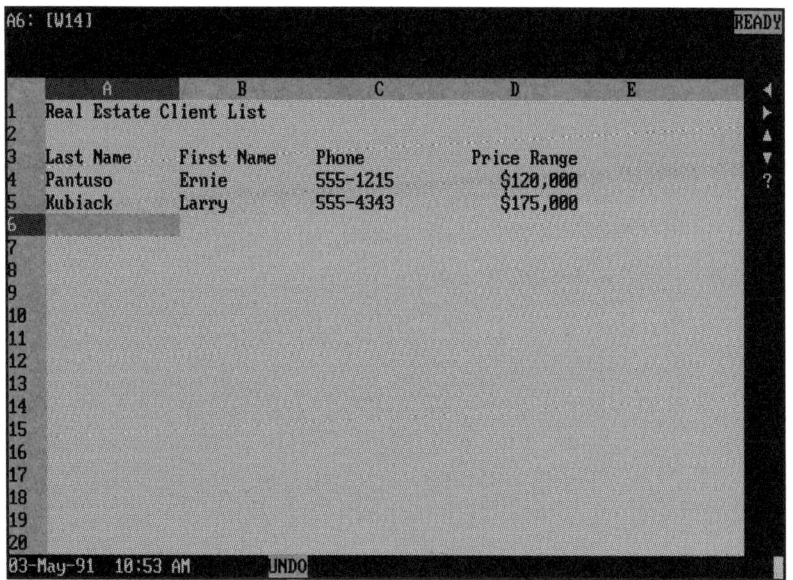

after

Be careful!
When you delete a row, you delete all the data in that row, including any data that is off-screen. Be sure to check the entire row before you delete it.

REVIEW

To delete a row

1. Move the cell pointer to the row that you want to delete.
2. Type /WDR to select the Worksheet Delete Row command.
3. Type the range address of the row(s) you want to delete.
4. Press Enter.

Remember...
When you delete a row, 1-2-3 recalculates any formulas that reference data in the row.

TASK

Insert a column

before

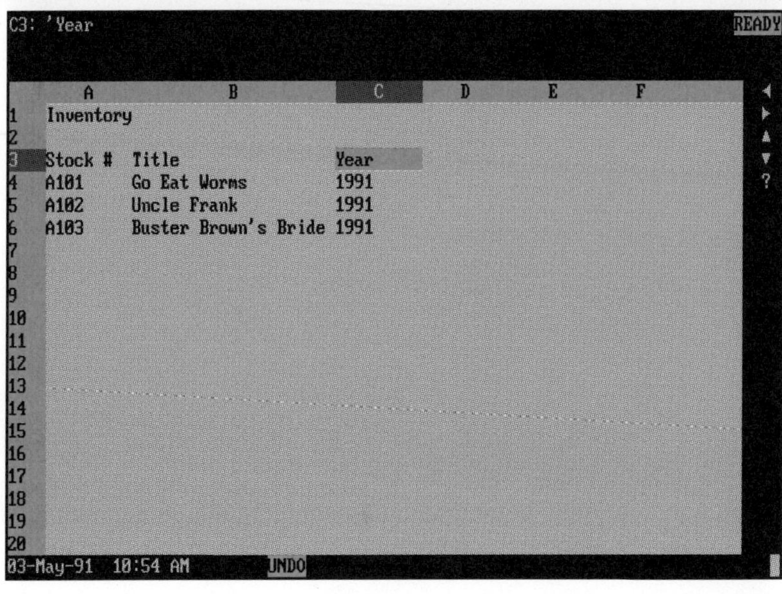

Oops!
To remove a new column, press the Alt-F4 key combination immediately after adding the column.

1. **Use the arrow keys to move the cell pointer to cell C3.**
   You will insert a column to the left of column C. You can position the cell pointer in any row in the column.

2. **Type /WI.**
   Typing /WI selects the Worksheet Insert command and displays two choices: Column and Row.

3. **Type C.**
   Typing C selects Column. You see the prompt `Enter column insert range: C3..C3`. C3 is the current cell.

4. **Press Enter.**
   Pressing Enter inserts one blank column.

   You also can insert more than one column. Type the range address for the number of columns that you want to insert. For example, you can type *C3..E3* to add three columns.

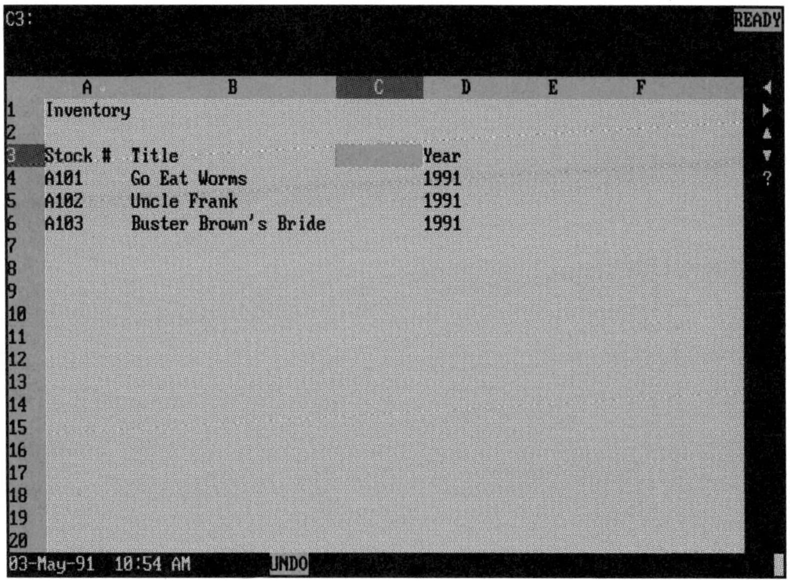

```
C3:                                                              READY

      A           B              C        D        E        F
1   Inventory
2
3   Stock #   Title                        Year
4   A101      Go Eat Worms                 1991
5   A102      Uncle Frank                  1991
6   A103      Buster Brown's Bride         1991
7
8
9
10
11
12
13
14
15
16
17
18
19
20
03-May-91  10:54 AM        UNDO
```

after

REVIEW

To insert a column

1. Move the cell pointer to the right of where you want the new column.
2. Type /WIC to select the Worksheet Insert Column command.
3. Type the range address of the column(s) that you want to insert.
4. Press Enter.

TASK

Delete a column

before

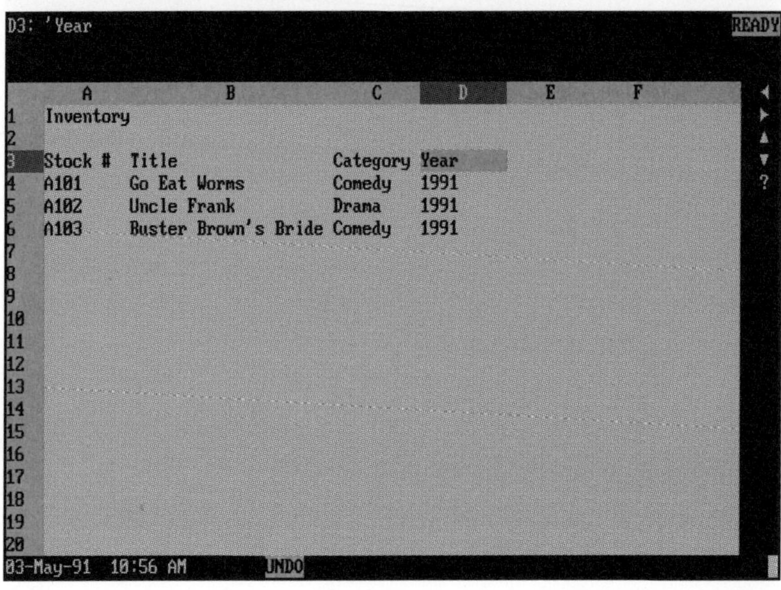

Oops!
To restore the deleted column, press the Alt-F4 key combination immediately after deleting the column.

1. Use the arrow keys to move the cell pointer to cell D3.

   Column D is the column that you want to delete. You can place the cell pointer in any row in the column.

2. Type **/WD**.

   Typing /WD selects the Worksheet Delete command and displays two choices: Column and Row.

3. Type **C**.

   Typing C selects Column. You see the prompt `Enter range of columns to delete: D3..D3`. D3 is the current cell.

4. Press **Enter**.

   Pressing Enter deletes the current column. You can delete more than one column. Simply type the range address for the columns that you want to delete. For example, type *D3..E3* to delete three columns.

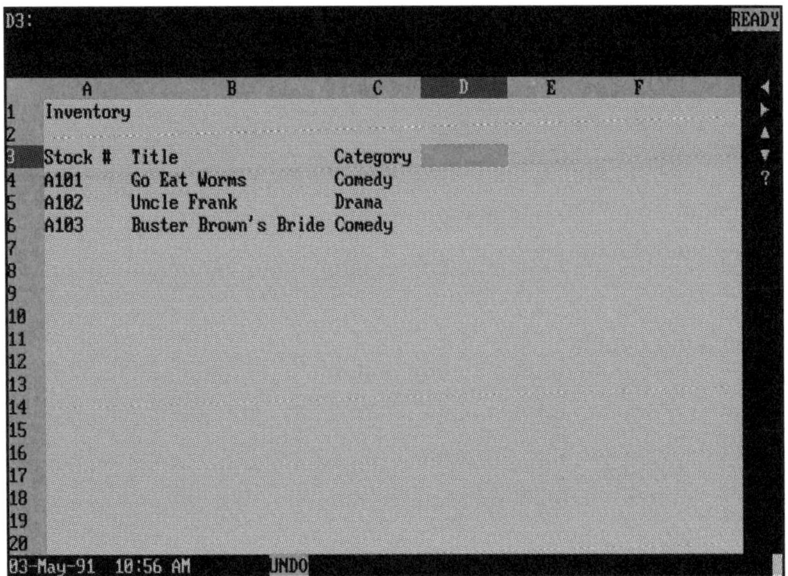

after

Be careful!
1-2-3 deletes all the data in a column when you delete the column. Check the entire column to be sure that you don't accidentally delete data that you need.

REVIEW

To delete a column

1. Move the cell pointer to the column that you want to delete.
2. Type /WDC to select the Worksheet Delete Column command.
3. Type the range address of the columns that you want to delete.

Remember...
When you delete a column, 1-2-3 recalculates any formulas that reference data in that column.

TASK

Hide columns

before

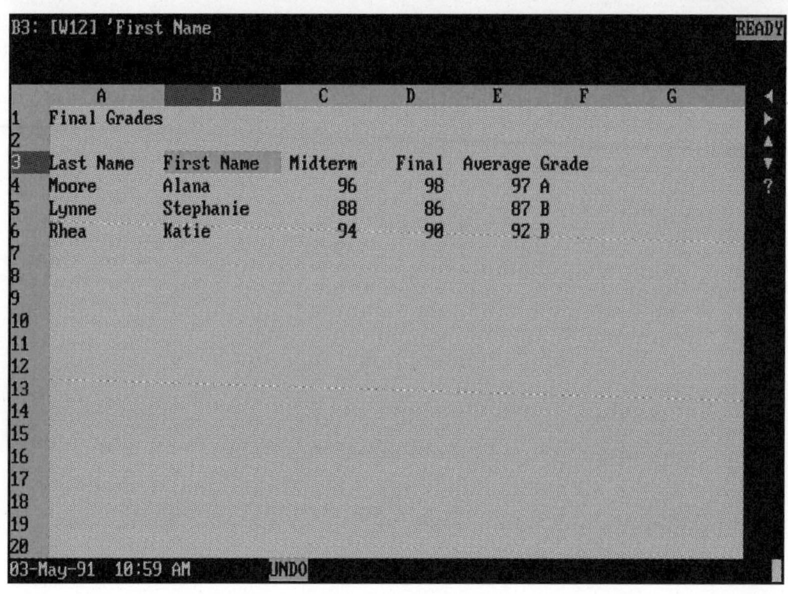

Oops!
To redisplay the column, press the Alt-F4 key combination immediately after hiding the column.

1. **Use the arrow keys to move the cell pointer to cell B3.**
   B3 is the first column that you want to hide. You can position the cell pointer in any row in the column.

2. **Type /WC.**
   Typing /WC selects the Worksheet Column command.

3. **Type H.**
   Typing H selects Hide. You see the prompt `Specify column to hide: B3`. B3 is the current cell.

4. **Type . (period).**
   Typing a period anchors the range. This means that it tells 1-2-3 to start the range with this cell.

5. **Press the → key three times.**
   Pressing the → key three times selects the range B3..E3. This is the range that you want to hide.

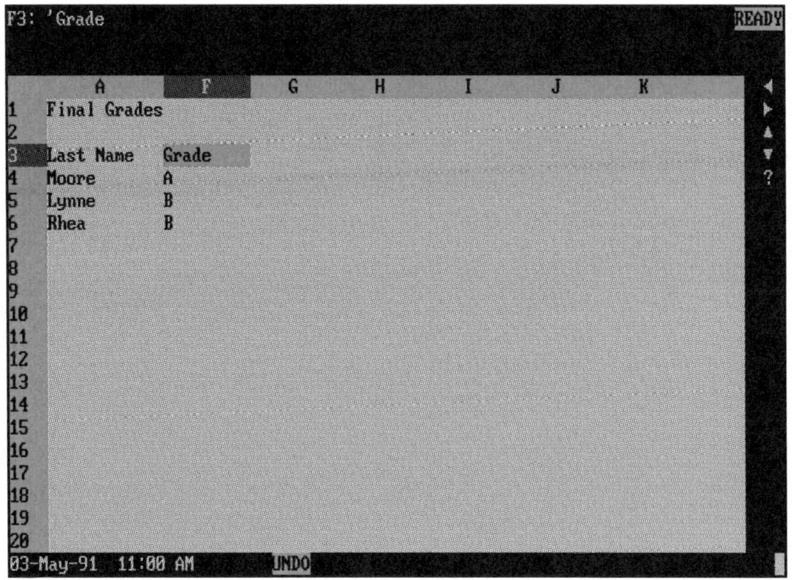

after

Redisplay hidden columns
To display hidden columns, type /WCD to select the Worksheet Column Display command. Then select the column(s) to redisplay.

6. Press **Enter**.

   Pressing Enter hides the columns on-screen. The information is still intact in the worksheet; you just cannot see it. You can see by the column numbering (A, F, G, and so on) that columns B–E have been hidden. The cell pointer remains in cell F3.

REVIEW

To hide columns

1. Move the cell pointer to the column that you want to hide.
2. Type **/WCH** to select the Worksheet Column Hide command.
3. Point to the range that you want or type the range address.
4. Press **Enter**.

Advanced Editing

This section covers the following tasks:

Use @SUM function

Copy a formula

Calculate an average

Copy a range

Erase a range

Move a range

Fill a range

Protect a worksheet

Name a range

List range names

Sort data

Search for data

Replace data

TASK

Use the @SUM function

before

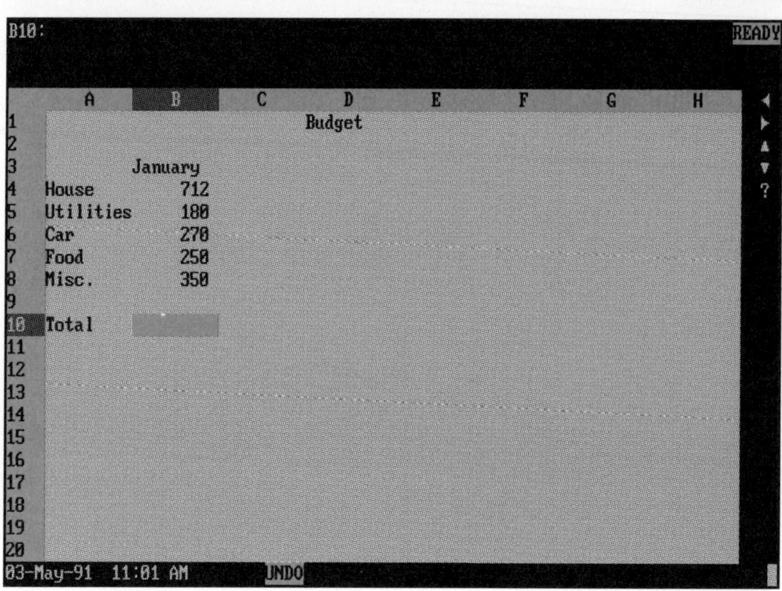

Oops!
If you get an error message while entering the function, you may not have typed the ending parenthesis. Press the Esc key and start over.

1. **Use the arrow keys to move the cell pointer to cell B10.**

   B10 is the cell that will contain the total.

2. **Type @SUM(.**

   @SUM is the name of the function that sums entries in a range automatically. You enter the range within the parentheses.

   The mode indicator changes to `VALUE`.

3. **Press the ↑ key six times.**

   When you press the ↑ key, the mode indicator changes to `POINT`. You can point to the cells that you want to include.

   Pressing the ↑ key six times moves the cell pointer to B4. This selection is the first cell in the range that you want to sum. You see `@SUM(B4` in the control panel.

4. **Type . (period).**

   Typing a period anchors the range. You see `@SUM(B4..B4` in the control panel.

5. **Press the ↓ key four times.**

   Pressing the ↓ key four times includes the range B4..B8 in the formula. The control panel displays `@SUM(B4..B8`.

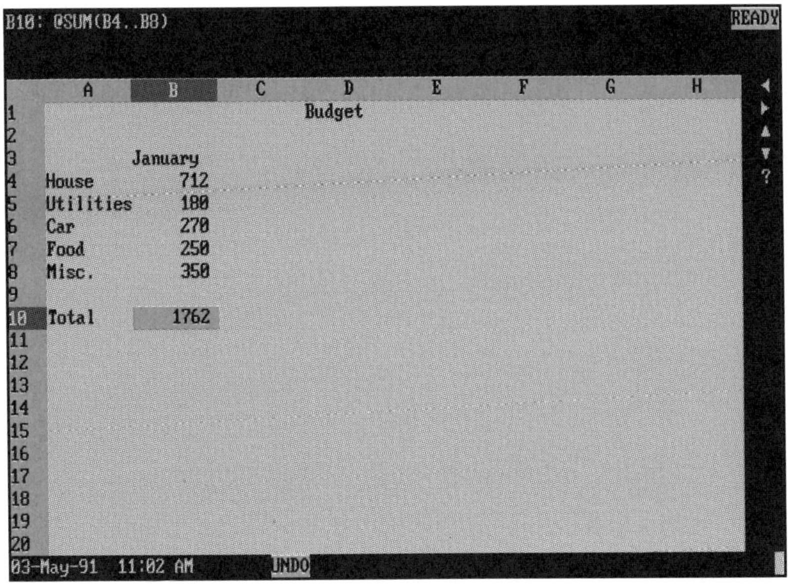

```
B10: @SUM(B4..B8)                                          READY

     A          B        C        D        E        F        G        H
1                               Budget
2
3            January
4  House          712
5  Utilities      180
6  Car            270
7  Food           250
8  Misc.          350
9
10 Total         1762
11
12
13
14
15
16
17
18
19
20
03-May-91  11:02 AM        UNDO
```

after

Why use the @SUM function?

The @SUM function sums a range. If you later insert or delete rows (or columns) within the range, the total is updated automatically.

6. Type) (right parenthesis).

   Typing a right parenthesis tells 1-2-3 that you are finished selecting the range. The range is inserted into the parentheses. You see `@SUM(B4..B8)` in the control panel. The cell pointer returns to B10, and the mode indicator changes to `VALUE`.

7. Press **Enter**.

   You see the results of the function in the cell (`1762`). You see the function (`@SUM(B4..B8)`) in the control panel.

REVIEW

To use the @SUM function

1. Move the cell pointer to the cell where you want the total to appear.
2. Type **@SUM(**.
3. Type or point to the first cell in the range that you want to sum.
4. Type . (period) and then point to the last cell in the range that you want to sum or type the range address.
5. Type).
6. Press **Enter**.

Use other functions

1-2-3 offers over 90 useful, timesaving functions. See the 1-2-3 manual or *Using 1-2-3 for DOS Release 2.3, Special Edition*, for more information.

TASK

Copy a formula

before

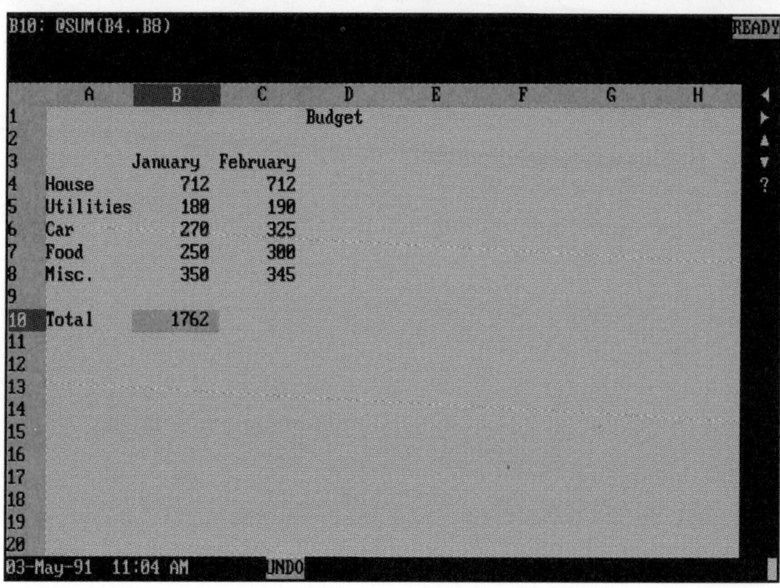

Oops!
To delete a formula that you copied, press the Alt-F4 key combination immediately after copying the formula.

1. **Use the arrow keys to move the cell pointer to cell B10.**

   Cell B10 contains the formula that you want to copy.

2. **Type /C.**

   Typing /C selects the Copy command. You see the prompt `Copy what? B10..B10`. B10 is the current cell—the cell that you want to copy. The mode indicator changes to `POINT`.

3. **Press Enter.**

   Pressing Enter confirms that you want to copy this cell.

   You see the prompt `To where? B10` in the control panel. B10 is the current cell.

4. **Press the → key once.**

   Pressing the → key once moves the cell pointer to cell C10. This is where you want the copy to appear.

5. **Press Enter.**

   The results of the formula appear in cell C10, and the cell pointer returns to cell B10.

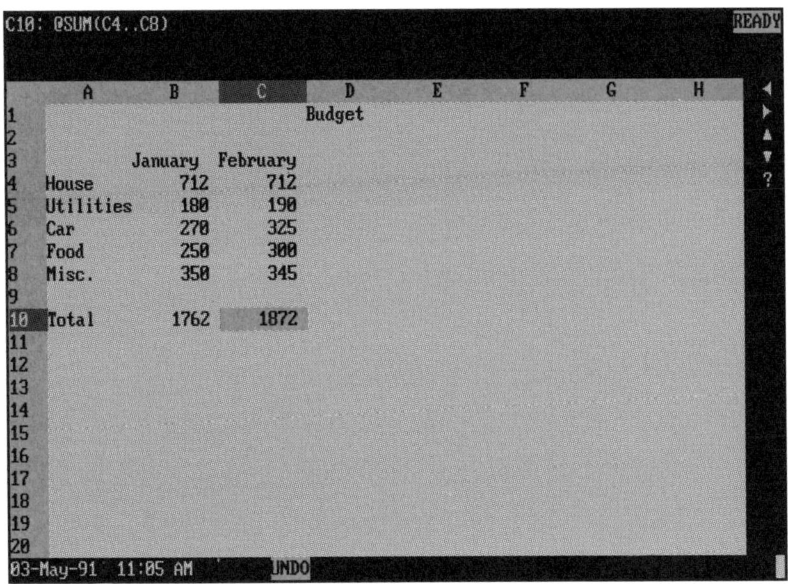

after

Copy a formula to a range
To copy a formula to an entire range, select a range when you see the prompt asking where to place the copy.

6. Press the → key **once**.

   Pressing the → key once moves the cell pointer back to cell C10.

   Notice that the control panel contains the formula `@SUM(C4..C8)`. This formula references the current column. The reference changes because of a 1-2-3 concept known as relative addressing. 1-2-3 automatically adjusts cell references when you copy a formula. For more information on relative addresses, see the 1-2-3 manual or *Using 1-2-3 for DOS Release 2.3,* Special Edition.

REVIEW

To copy a formula

1. Move the cell pointer to the cell that contains the formula you want to copy.
2. Type /C to select the Copy command.
3. Press **Enter** to specify the current cell as the source or type a new source cell.
4. Point to or type the destination cell.
5. Press **Enter**.

Copy a range
You can copy a range rather than a single cell. See *TASK: Copy a range.*

TASK

Calculate an average

before

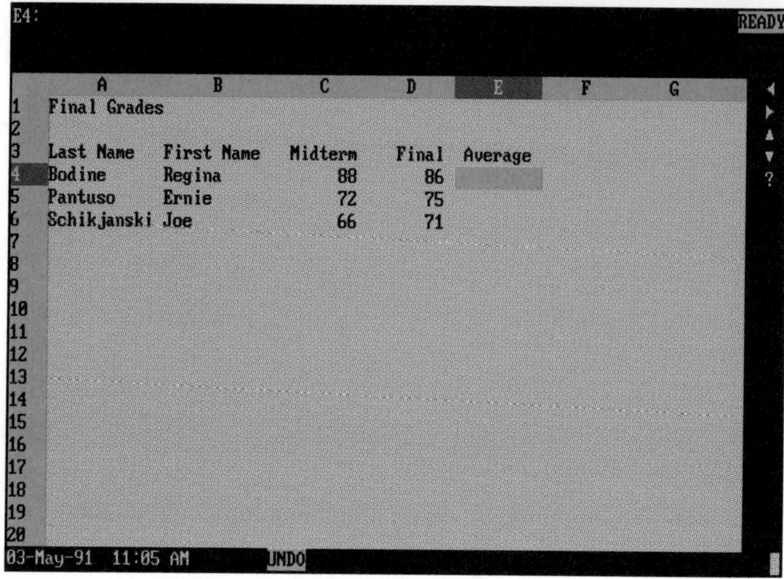

Oops!
If you get an error message while entering the function, you may not have typed the ending parenthesis. Press the Esc key and start over.

1. **Use the arrow keys to move the cell pointer to cell E4.**

   E4 will contain the function that calculates the average. The mode indicator displays `READY`, which tells you that 1-2-3 is ready to accept an entry.

2. **Type @AVG(.**

   @AVG is the name of the function that automatically averages entries in a range. You enter the range that you want to average within the parentheses. The mode indicator changes to `VALUE`.

3. **Press the ← key twice.**

   When you press the ← key, the mode indicator changes to `POINT`. This indicator reminds you that you can point to the range.

   Pressing the ← key twice moves the cell pointer to C4. This is the first cell in the range that you want to average. You see `@AVG(C4` in the control panel.

4. **Type . (period).**

   Typing a period anchors the range. You see `@AVG(C4..C4` in the control panel.

5. **Press the → key once.**

   Pressing the → key once includes the range C4..D4 in the formula. You see `@AVG(C4..D4` in the control panel.

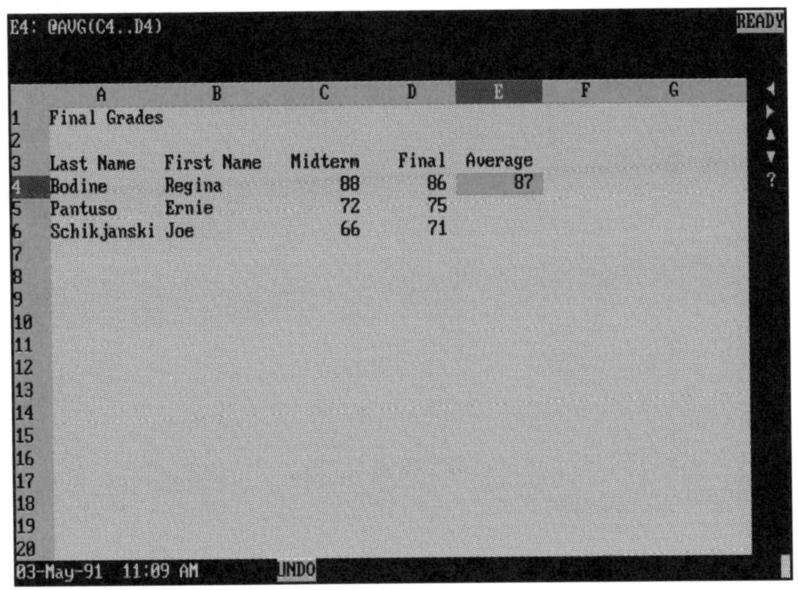

after

Use other functions
1-2-3 offers over 90 useful, timesaving functions. See the 1-2-3 manual or *Using 1-2-3 for DOS Release 2.3,* Special Edition, for more information.

6. Type) (right parenthesis).

   Typing a right parenthesis tells 1-2-3 that you are finished selecting the range. The range is inserted into the parentheses. You now see @AVG(C4..D4) in the control panel. The cell pointer returns to cell E4, and the mode indicator changes to VALUE.

7. Press **Enter**.

   The result of the function appears in the cell (87). The control panel display the function @AVG(C4..D4).

   To complete the worksheet, you can copy this formula to the other rows in the column. See *TASK: Copy a formula*.

REVIEW

To calculate an average

1. Move the cell pointer to the cell where you want the average to appear.
2. Type @AVG(.
3. Point to the range or type the range address.
4. Type).
5. Press **Enter**.

Copy a range

before

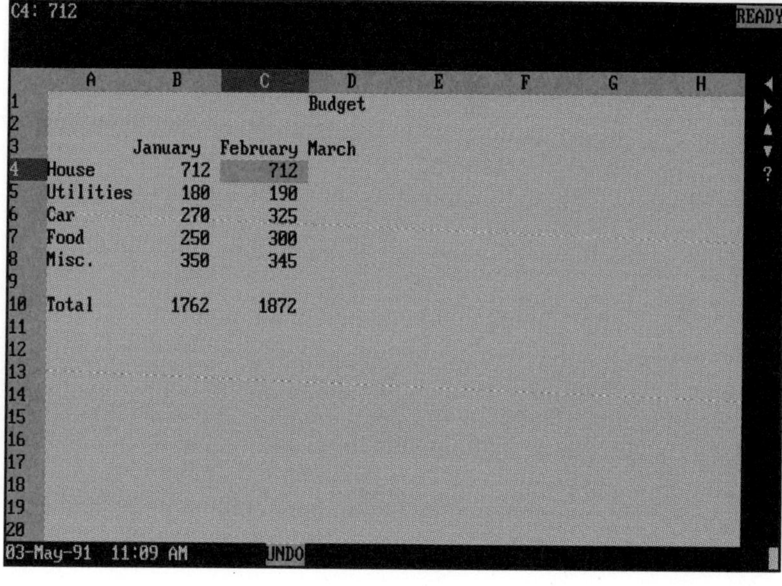

Oops!
To delete the copy, press the Alt-F4 key combination immediately after making the copy.

1. **Use the arrow keys to move the cell pointer to cell C4.**

   C4 is the first cell in the range that you want to copy.

2. **Type /C.**

   Typing /C selects the Copy command. You see the prompt `Copy what? C4..C4`. C4 is the current cell. The mode indicator displays `POINT`, which reminds you that you can point to the range.

3. **Press the ↓ key six times.**

   Pressing the ↓ key six times selects the range C4..C10. This is the range that you want to copy.

4. **Press Enter.**

   Pressing Enter confirms the range. You see the prompt `To where? C4`. C4 is the current cell.

5. **Press the → key once.**

   Pressing the → key once moves the cell pointer to D4. D4 is the first cell of the area where you want to place the copied range. The copied range takes the same shape and space as the original.

C4: 712 READY

	A	B	C	D	E	F	G	H
1				Budget				
2								
3		January	February	March				
4	House	712	712	712				
5	Utilities	180	190	190				
6	Car	270	325	325				
7	Food	250	300	300				
8	Misc.	350	345	345				
9								
10	Total	1762	1872	1872				
11								
12								
13								
14								
15								
16								
17								
18								
19								
20								

03-May-91 11:10 AM UNDO

after

Caution!
Be careful not to overwrite existing data. Select a blank range for the copy.

6. Press **Enter**.

   Pressing Enter copies the range to the new location. The cell pointer returns to cell C4.

REVIEW

To copy a range

1. Move the cell pointer to the first cell in the range that you want to copy.
2. Type /C to select the Copy command.
3. Point to or type the address of the range that you want to copy.
4. Press **Enter**.
5. Point to or type the new destination.
6. Press **Enter**.

TASK

Erase a range

before

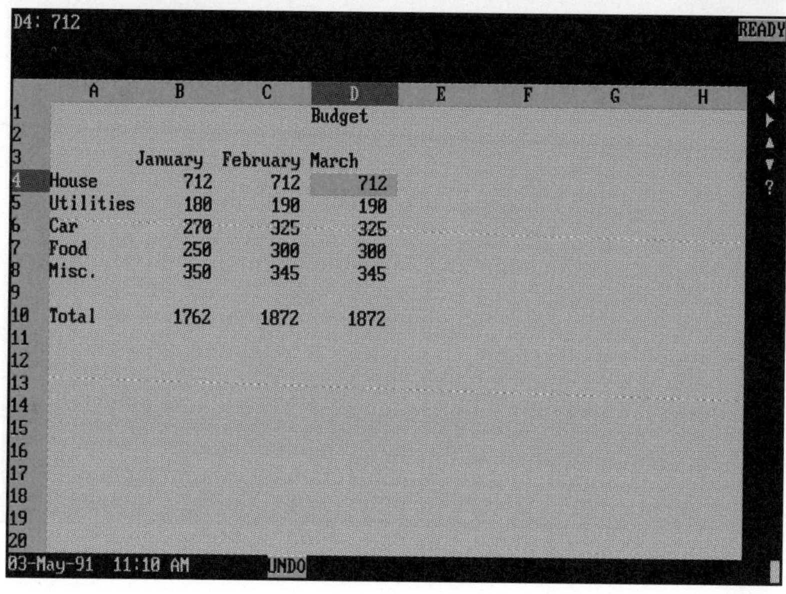

Oops!
To restore a range, press the Alt-F4 key combination immediately after erasing a range.

1. **Use the arrow keys to move the cell pointer to cell D4.**

   D4 is the first cell in the range that you want to erase.

2. **Type /RE.**

   Typing /RE selects the Range Erase command. You see the prompt `Enter range to erase: D4..D4`. D4 is the current cell. You are now in `POINT` mode.

3. **Press the ↓ key four times.**

   Pressing the ↓ key four times selects the range D4..D8. This is the range that you want to erase.

4. **Press Enter.**

   Pressing Enter erases the range. The cell pointer returns to D4.

   You now can enter new values in the range.

   If you erase cells that were included in a formula, the formula is recalculated. Notice that the formula in cell D10 is recalculated and is now zero.

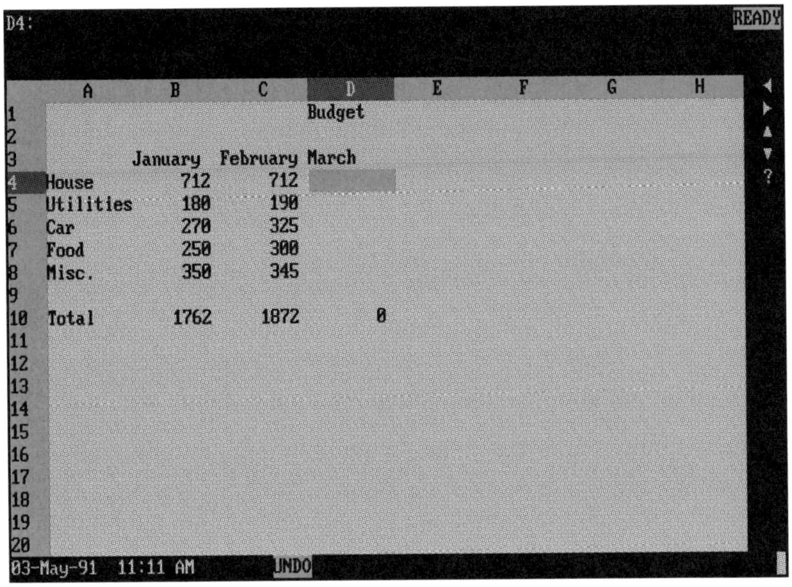

```
D4:                                                                READY

        A           B           C           D           E           F           G           H
1                                        Budget
2
3                January    February    March
4   House             712         712
5   Utilities         180         190
6   Car               270         325
7   Food              250         300
8   Misc.             350         345
9
10  Total            1762        1872            0
11
12
13
14
15
16
17
18
19
20
03-May-91   11:11 AM          UNDO
```

after

When you erase a range...
Erasing the range removes only the data in the range, not the formats or the cell protection.

REVIEW

To erase a range

1. Move the cell pointer to the first cell in the range that you want to erase.
2. Type /RE to select the Range Erase command.
3. Point to the range or type the address of the range that you want to erase.
4. Press Enter.

Be careful!
Before you erase a range, make sure that you will not need any of the data in the range.

TASK

Move a range

before

```
C3: 'CATEGORY                                              READY

     A        B        C        D      E      F      G      H
1  Check Register
2
3  DATE     PAYEE    CATEGORY AMOUNT
4  04-04    Atlas    Grocery   $69.32
5  04-04    Target   Household $51.41
6  04-05    Mortgage House    $712.00
7
8
9
10
11
12
13
14
15
16
17
18
19
20
03-May-91  11:24 AM         UNDO
```

Oops!
To move the range back to its original location, press the Alt-F4 key combination. You must press these keys before you delete the column.

1. **Use the arrow keys to move the cell pointer to cell C3.**

   C3 is the first cell in the range that you want to move.

2. **Type /M.**

   Typing /M selects the Move command. You see the prompt `Move what? C3..C3`. C3 is the current cell. You now are in `POINT` mode.

3. **Press the ↓ key three times.**

   Pressing the ↓ key three times selects the range C3..C6. This is the range that you want to move.

4. **Press Enter.**

   Pressing Enter confirms the selected range. You see the prompt `To where? C3`. C3 is the current cell.

5. **Press the → key twice.**

   Pressing the → key twice moves the cell pointer to E3. E3 is the first cell of the area where you want to place the range. The range has the same shape and takes the same space as the original. Be careful not to overwrite existing data.

6. **Press Enter.**

   Pressing Enter moves the range to the new location. The original location is blank. The cell pointer returns to C3.

   You can use this process to rearrange the worksheet. Next delete column C. You do not have to delete a column when you move a range.

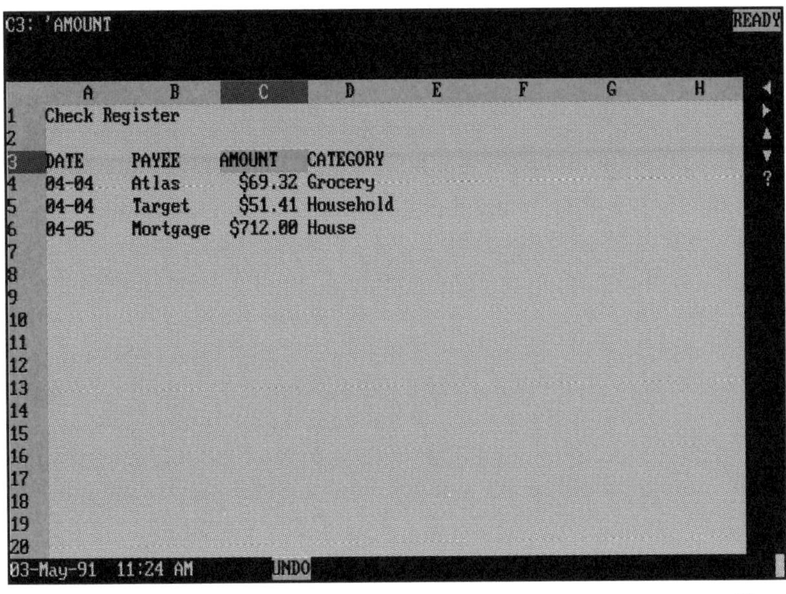

after

7. Type **/WDC**.

   Typing /WDC selects the Worksheet Delete Column command. You see the prompt `Enter range of columns to delete: C3..C3.`

8. Press **Enter**.

   Pressing Enter confirms the command, and the column is deleted.

REVIEW

To move a range

1. Move the cell pointer to the first cell in the range that you want to move.
2. Type **/M** to select the Move command.
3. Point to the range or type the address of the range that you want to move.
4. Press **Enter**.
5. Point to or type the destination.
6. Press **Enter**.

TASK

Fill a range

before

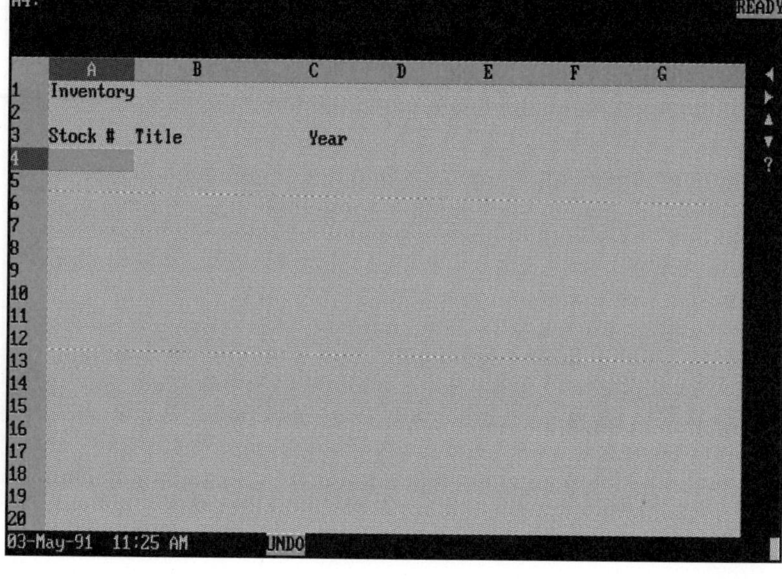

Oops!
To undo a fill, press the Alt-F4 key combination immediately after performing the fill.

1. **Use the arrow keys to place the cell pointer in cell A4.**
   A4 is the first cell that you want to fill with data.

2. **Type /DF.**
   Typing /DF selects the Data Fill command. You see the prompt `Enter fill range: A4`. A4 is the current cell. You are now in `POINT` mode.

3. **Type . (period).**
   Typing a period anchors the range.

4. **Press the ↓ key three times.**
   Pressing the ↓ key three times selects A4..A7. This is the range that you want to fill.

5. **Press Enter.**
   Pressing Enter confirms the range to be filled. You are prompted to specify the start value. The default is 0.

6. **Type 100.**
   100 is the starting number for the range fill.

7. **Press Enter.**
   Pressing Enter confirms the starting number. You are prompted for the step value. The default is 1.

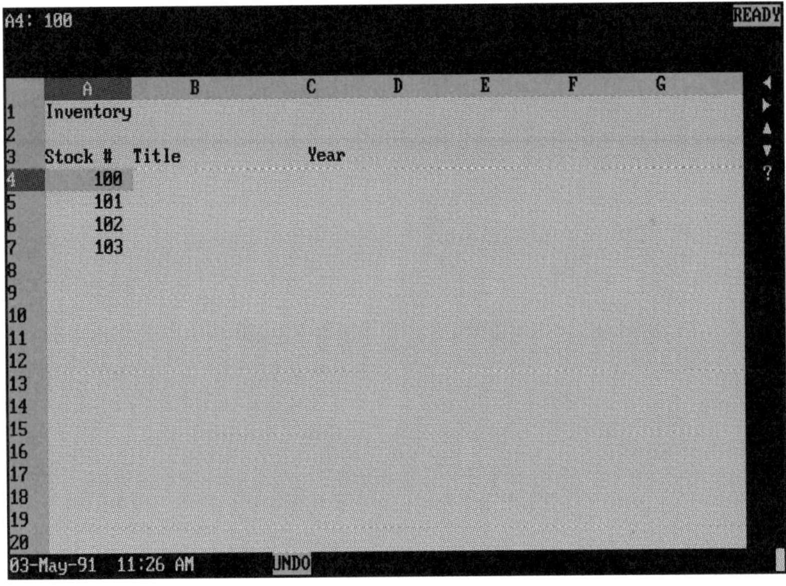

after

8. Press **Enter**.

   Pressing Enter accepts the default value of 1. This step tells 1-2-3 to increment the number by one. You are prompted for the stop value. The default is 8191.

9. Press **Enter**.

   Because you have already specified the range, you do not have to specify the stop value. 1-2-3 fills only the selected range.

   On-screen, the range that you selected fills with numbers that begin with 100 and increment by 1. The cell pointer returns to cell A4.

REVIEW

To fill a range

1. Move the cell pointer to the first cell in the range that you want to fill with data.
2. Type **/DF** to select the Data Fill command.
3. Point to or type the address of the range that you want to fill and press **Enter**.
4. Type a start value and press **Enter**.
5. Type a step value and press **Enter**.
6. Type a stop value and press **Enter**.

Protect a worksheet

before

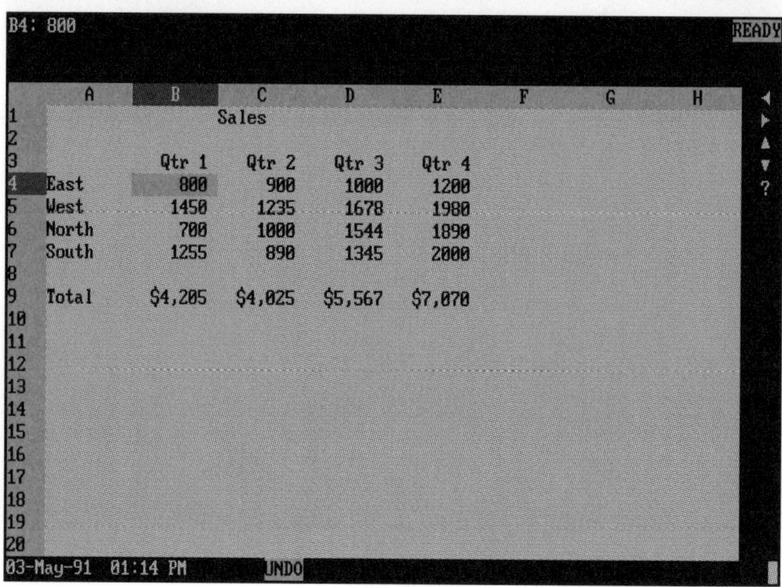

B4: 800
READY
A
B
C
D
E
F
G
H
Sales
Qtr 1 Qtr 2 Qtr 3 Qtr 4
East 800 900 1000 1200
West 1450 1235 1678 1980
North 700 1000 1544 1890
South 1255 890 1345 2000
Total $4,205 $4,025 $5,567 $7,070
03-May-91 01:14 PM
UNDO

Oops!
To undo the protection, press the Alt-F4 key combination immediately.

1. **Type /WG.**

   Typing /WG selects the Worksheet Global command. The Global Settings dialog box appears. Notice that `Protection on` is the first entry.

2. **Type P.**

   Typing P selects Protection. You see two choices in the control panel: Enable and Disable.

3. **Type E.**

   Typing E selects Enable and turns on worksheet protection. You must turn on protection for the cells to be protected.

   You are returned to the worksheet. You see `PR` in the control panel. All the cells are now protected. You cannot make any changes or delete any of the entries in the worksheet.

   You will now test the cell protection to make sure it is on.

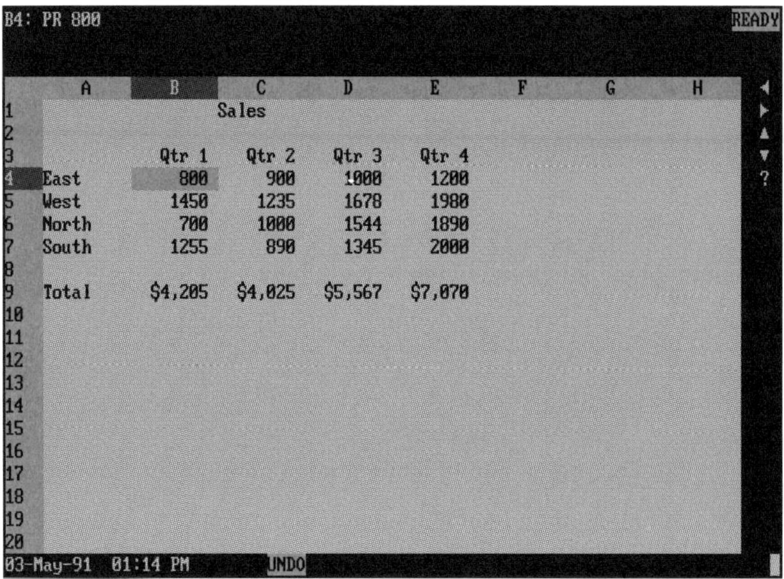

after

Unprotect all cells
To unprotect all cells, type /WGPD to select Worksheet Global Protection Disable.

4. Move the cell pointer to cell B4, type **1**, and press **Enter**.

   You see the message `Error Protected cell`.

5. Press **Esc**.

   Pressing the Esc key clears the message.

REVIEW

To protect a worksheet

Type **/WGPE** to select the Worksheet Global Protection Enable command.

Unprotect a range
To unprotect a range, type /RU to select the Range Unprot command. Point to or type the address of the range and press Enter.

TASK

Name a range

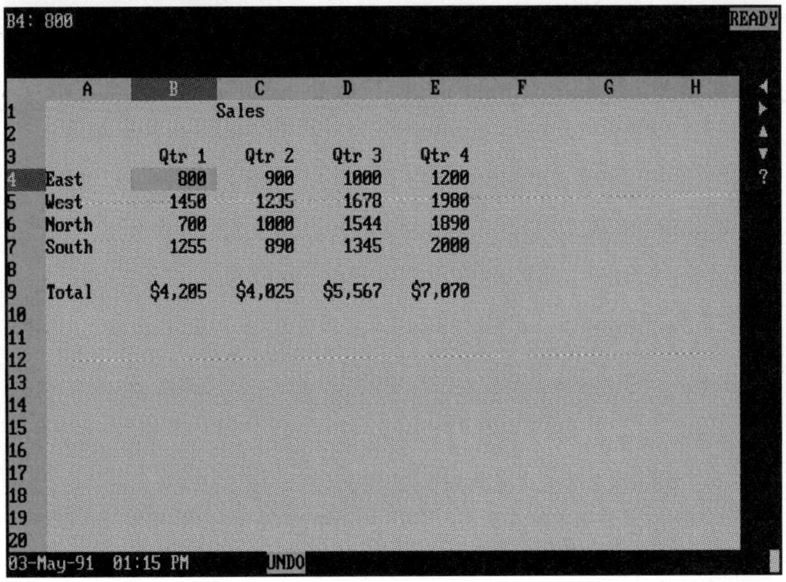

Oops!
To delete the name, press the Alt-F4 key combination immediately after creating the name.

before

B4: 800 READY

	A	B	C	D	E	F	G	H
1			Sales					
2								
3		Qtr 1	Qtr 2	Qtr 3	Qtr 4			
4	East	800	900	1000	1200			
5	West	1450	1235	1678	1980			
6	North	700	1000	1544	1890			
7	South	1255	890	1345	2000			
8								
9	Total	$4,205	$4,025	$5,567	$7,070			
10								
11								
12								
13								
14								
15								
16								
17								
18								
19								
20								

03-May-91 01:15 PM UNDO

1. **Use the arrow keys to move the cell pointer to cell B4.**
   B4 is the first cell in the range that you want to name. Remember that a range can be any rectangular area—including just one cell.

2. **Type /RN.**
   Typing /RN selects the Range Name command. You see a list of choices in the control panel.

3. **Type C.**
   Typing C selects Create. You see the prompt `Enter name:`.

4. **Type QTR1.**
   QTR1 is the name that you want to assign to this range. You can type up to 15 characters. As a general rule, use only alphanumeric characters.

5. **Press Enter.**
   You see the prompt `Enter range: B4..B4`. B4 is the current cell.

6. **Press the ↓ key three times.**
   Pressing the ↓ key three times selects the range B4..B7.

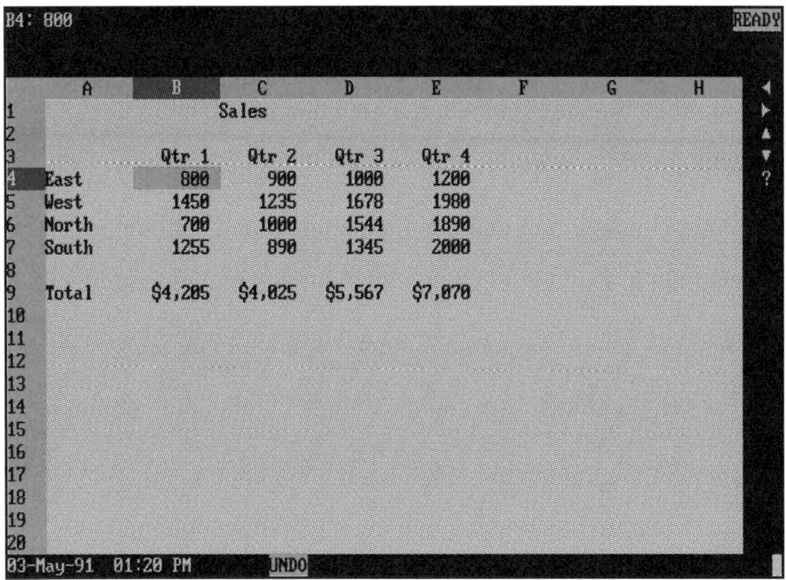

after

Delete the name
You can delete the name by typing /RND to select the Range Name Delete command. Highlight the name to delete and press Enter.

7. Press **Enter**.

   Pressing Enter confirms the selected range. Nothing changes on-screen. The cell and control panel appear the same. To display range names, see *TASK: List range names*.

   The name is saved with the worksheet when you save the worksheet.

REVIEW

To name a range

1. Move the cell pointer to the first cell in the range that you want to name.
2. Type /**RNC** to select the Range Name Create command.
3. Type a name.
4. Press **Enter**.
5. Point to the range or type the range address.
6. Press **Enter**.

Why use names?
Names are easy to remember. You can use range names in formulas, and you can use the GoTo key to move to a named range quickly.

TASK

List range names

before

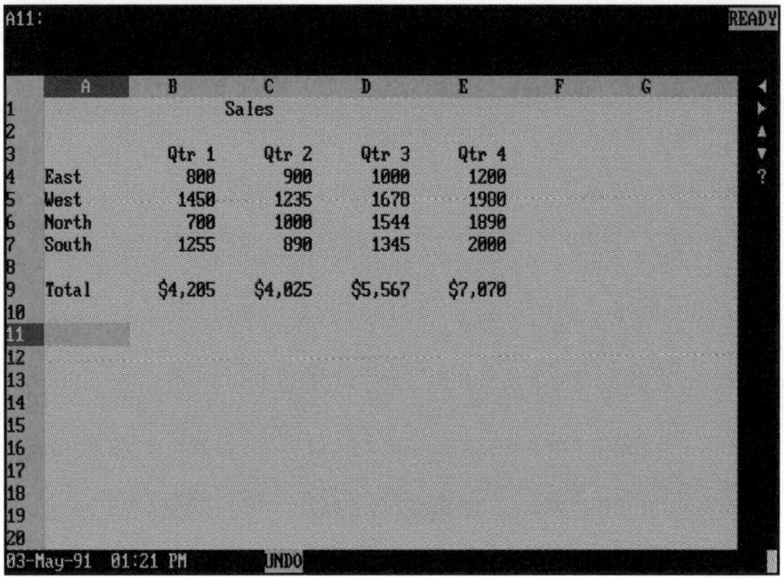

```
A11:                                                              READY

     A        B         C         D         E         F         G
1                     Sales
2
3                  Qtr 1     Qtr 2     Qtr 3     Qtr 4
4   East             800       900      1000      1200
5   West            1450      1235      1670      1900
6   North            700      1000      1544      1890
7   South           1255       890      1345      2000
8
9   Total         $4,205    $4,025    $5,567    $7,070
10
11
12
13
14
15
16
17
18
19
20
03-May-91  01:21 PM        UNDO
```

Oops!
To delete the list, press the Alt-F4 key combination immediately after you create the list.

1. **Name the ranges.**

   To list range names, you first must create them. See *TASK: Name a range* for information on this step.

2. **Use the arrow keys to move the cell pointer to cell A11.**

   A11 is the first cell where you want the list of names to appear. The list of names is two columns wide and as many rows deep as there are names. Be sure not to position the table where you may overwrite any data.

3. **Type /RN.**

   Typing /RN selects the Range Name command.

4. **Type T.**

   Typing T selects the Table command. You see the prompt `Enter range for table: A11..A11`. **A11 is the current cell.**

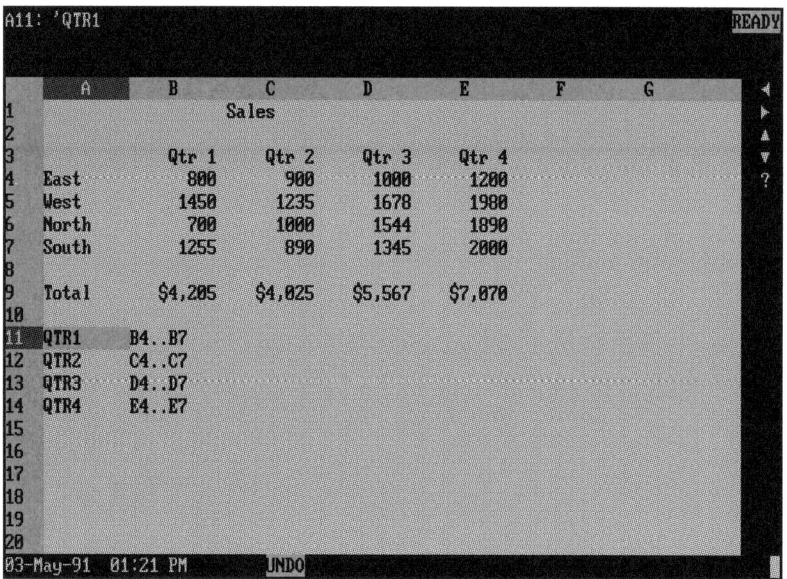

after

5. Press **Enter**.

   Pressing Enter inserts the beginning of the table in cell A11. On-screen you see a two-column list. The first column lists the range names; the second column lists the cell address for the range.

Create range names
If you don't see any names in the list, it may be because you haven't created any. You must create names before you can list them.

REVIEW

To list range names

1. Move the cell pointer to the first cell in the range that will contain the list.
2. Type **/RNT** to select the Range Name Table command.
3. Press **Enter** to insert the table starting in the current cell. Or type the range address where you want to insert the table and press **Enter**.

Erase a list of range names
If you decide that you do not want a list of range names, you can erase the range. See *TASK: Erase a range*.

TASK

Sort data

(Part 1 of 2)

before

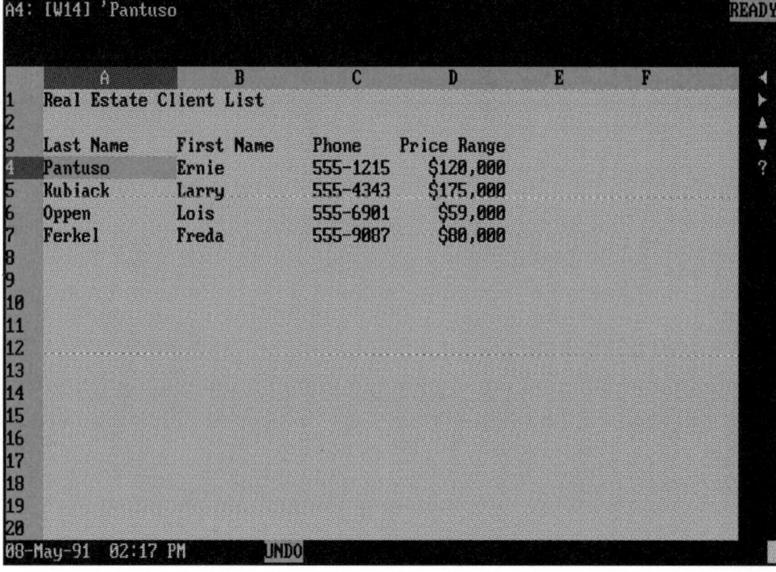

Oops!
If you did not select the correct range, press the Esc key and start over.

Sorting data is a two-part process. The first part, Select the range, is covered on these two pages. Turn the page for the second part, Perform the sort.

1. Use the arrow keys to move the cell pointer to cell A4.
   A4 is the first cell in the range that you want to sort.

2. Type **/DS**.
   Typing /DS selects the Data Sort command. You see the Sort Settings dialog box in the middle of the screen and a list of menu options in the control panel.

3. Type **D**.
   Typing D selects the Data-Range command. You see the prompt `Enter data range: A4`. A4 is the current cell. The Sort Settings dialog box disappears, and 1-2-3 enters `POINT` mode.

4. Type **.** (period).
   Typing a period anchors the range.

5. Press the ↓ key **three times**.
   Pressing the ↓ key three times highlights A4..A7. This is the range that you want to sort.

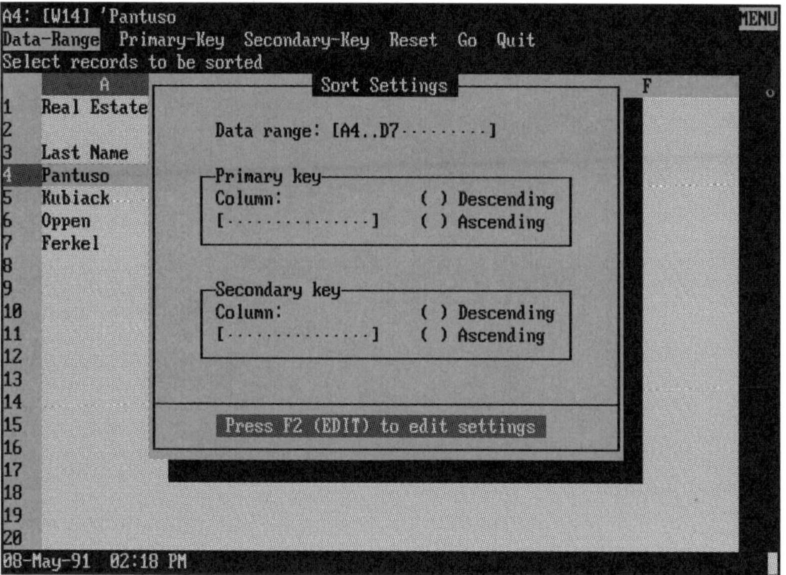

after

Save your worksheet You should save your worksheet before you begin to sort data. Then if you make a mistake, you can go back to the original version.

6. Press the → key **three times**.

   Pressing the → key three times extends the range to A4..E7. If other data in the row is connected to that column, be sure to include the entire range—not just the column you want to sort. If you select only the column, the entries become mismatched.

   Be sure to select only the data and not any row or column headings.

7. Press **Enter**.

   Pressing Enter confirms the selected range. The dialog box appears again and lists the range. You see the menu choices listed in the control panel.

REVIEW

To sort data

(Part 1 of 2)

1. Move the cell pointer to the first cell in the range that you want to sort.
2. Type **/DS** to select the Data Sort command.
3. Type **D** to select Data-Range.
4. Point to the range that you want to sort or type the range address.
5. Press **Enter**.

Sort numbers You can use this same procedure to sort numbers.

Sort data

(Part 2 of 2)

before

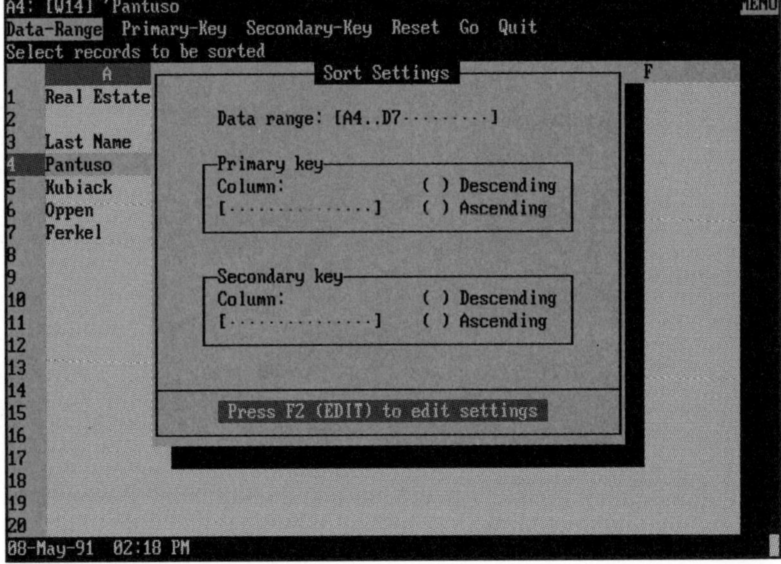

Oops!
If the sort did not work as planned, press the Alt-F4 key combination immediately to restore the range to its original order.

Sorting data is a two-part process. The first part, Select the range, is covered on the preceding two pages. These two pages cover the second part, Perform the sort.

1. **Type P.**

   Typing P selects Primary-Key. This selection tells 1-2-3 how to sort the range. You see the prompt `Primary sort key: A4`. **A4** is the current cell.

2. **Press Enter.**

   Pressing Enter confirms that A4 is the category on which you want to begin the sort. You can select any row in this column.

   You see the prompt `Sort order (A or D): D`.

3. **Type A.**

   Typing A selects ascending order.

4. **Press Enter.**

   Pressing Enter confirms the sort order. You see the selections in the dialog box. The control panel lists the menu choices.

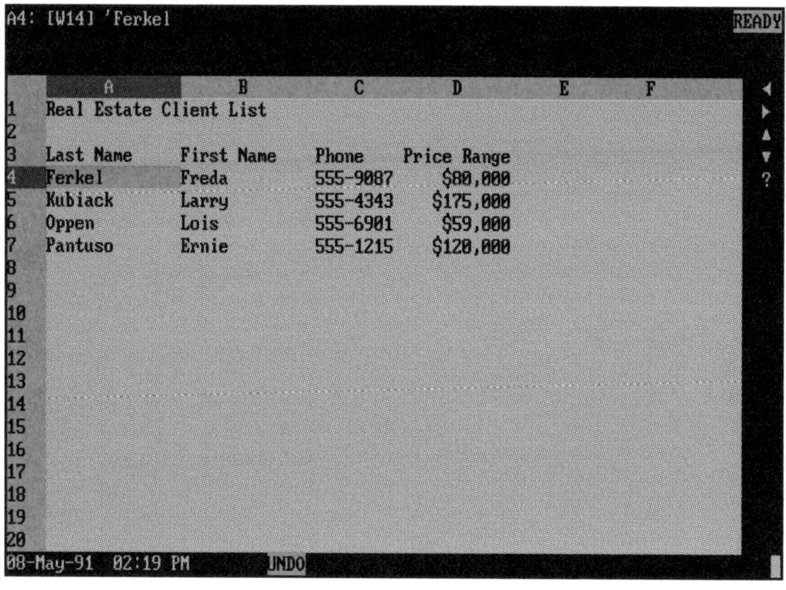

after

Save your worksheet
You should save your worksheet before you sort the data. Then if you make a mistake, you can go back to the original version.

5. Type **G**.

   Typing G selects Go from the menu. The data is sorted in alphabetical order by last name. The cell pointer returns to cell A4.

REVIEW

To sort data

(Part 2 of 2)

1. Type **P** to select Primary-Key.
2. Type or point to the column to use as the sort key.
3. Press **Enter**.
4. Type **A** or **D** to specify ascending or descending order.
5. Press **Enter**.
6. Type **G** to select Go.

Sort numbers
You can use this same procedure to sort numbers.

TASK

Search for data

before

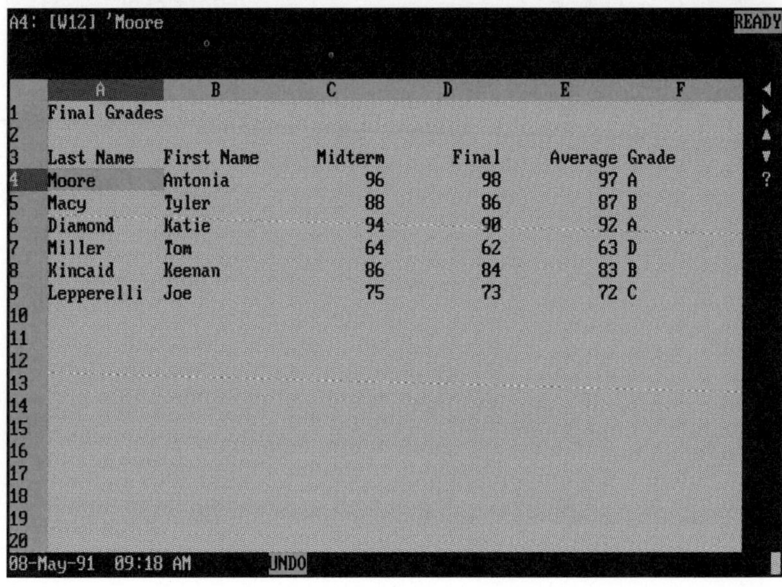

A4: [W12] 'Moore
READY
A B C D E F
1 Final Grades
2
3 Last Name First Name Midterm Final Average Grade
4 Moore Antonia 96 98 97 A
5 Macy Tyler 88 86 87 B
6 Diamond Katie 94 90 92 A
7 Miller Tom 64 62 63 D
8 Kincaid Keenan 86 84 83 B
9 Lepperelli Joe 75 73 72 C
10
11
12
13
14
15
16
17
18
19
20
08-May-91 09:18 AM
UNDO

Oops!
To exit the search, press the Esc key.

1. **Use the arrow keys to move the cell pointer to cell A4.**
   A4 is the first cell in the range that you want to search.
2. **Type /RS.**
   Typing /RS selects the Range Search command.
3. **Type . (period).**
   Typing a period anchors the range.
4. **Press the ↓ key five times.**
   Pressing the ↓ key five times selects the range A4..A9.
5. **Press Enter.**
   Pressing Enter confirms the selected range. You see the prompt `Enter string to search for:`.
6. **Type Diamond.**
   Diamond is the text that you want to find. This is called a search string.
7. **Press Enter.**
   Pressing Enter confirms the search string.
8. **Type L.**
   Typing L tells 1-2-3 to just search labels (or text) in the worksheet.
9. **Type F.**
   Typing F selects Find. The cell pointer moves to the first occurrence of the search string.

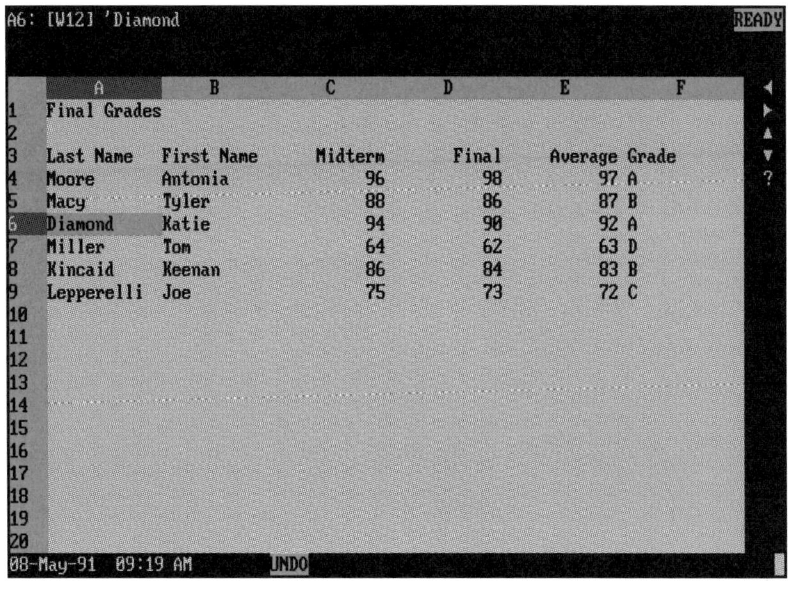

after

What is a search string? The search string is a set of characters, such as a word or value, for which 1-2-3 looks in search and replace operations.

10. Type **N**.

    Typing N tells 1-2-3 to find the next match. 1-2-3 cannot find any more occurrences of the text; you see the message `No more matching strings`.

11. Press **Esc**.

    Pressing the Esc key clears the error message.

REVIEW

To search for data

1. Move the cell pointer to the first cell in the range that you want to search.
2. Type /**RS** to select the Range Search command.
3. Point to the range or type the range address.
4. Press **Enter**.
5. Type the desired search string and press **Enter**.
6. Type **F**, **L**, or **B** to search for Formulas, Labels, or Both.
7. Type **F** to select Find.
8. Type **N** to select Next and find the next match.
9. Press **Esc** to quit the search.

Replace data

(Part 1 of 2)

before

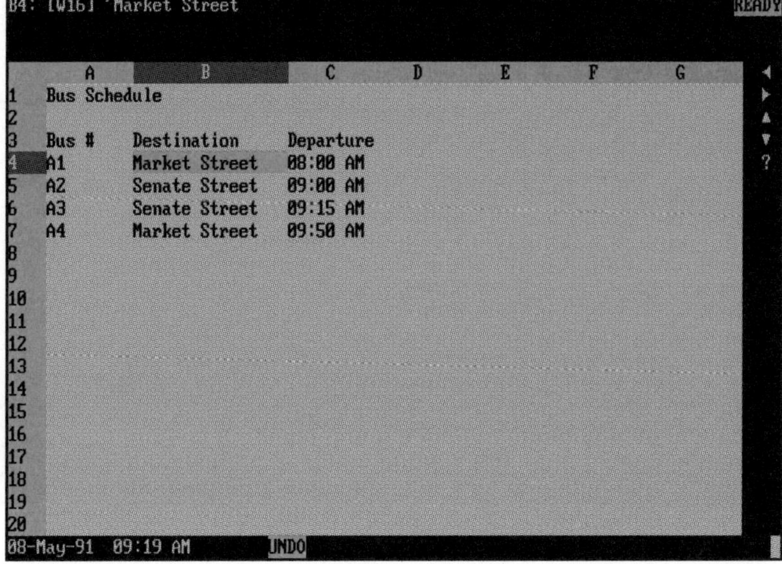

Oops!
If you select the wrong range, press the Esc key and start over.

Replacing data is a two-part process. The first part, Enter search range and string, is covered on these two pages. Turn the page for the second part, Make replacements.

1. **Use the arrow keys to move the cell pointer to cell B4.**
   B4 is the first cell in the range that you want to search.

2. **Type /RS.**
   Typing /RS selects the Range Search command. You see the prompt `Enter range to search: B4`. B4 is the current cell. 1-2-3 enters `POINT` mode.

3. **Type . (period).**
   Typing a period anchors the range.

4. **Press the ↓ key three times.**
   Pressing the ↓ key three times selects the range B4..B7. This is the range that you are searching.

5. **Press Enter.**
   Pressing Enter confirms the selected range. You see the prompt `Enter string to search for:`.

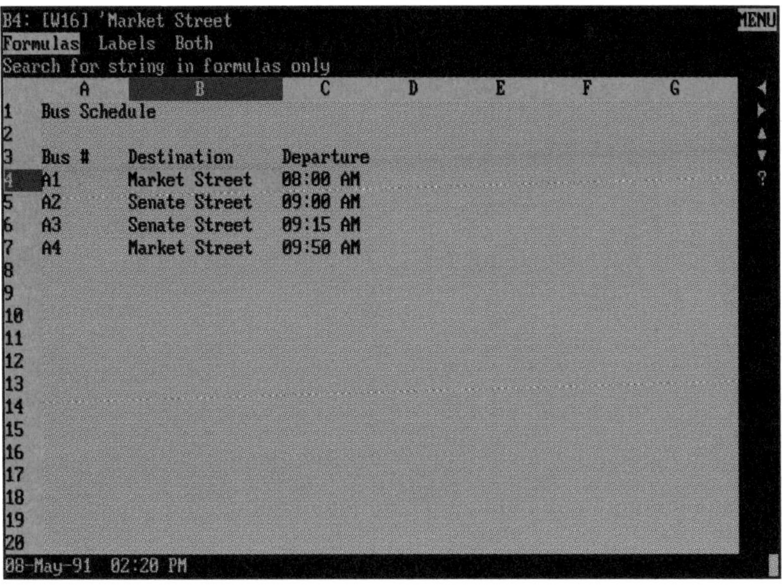

after

What is a search string? The search string is a set of characters, such as a word or value, for which 1-2-3 looks in search and replace operations.

6. Type **Senate Street**.

   Senate Street is the text that you want to find. This is called a search string.

7. Press **Enter**.

   Pressing Enter confirms the search string. You see these choices in the control panel: Formulas, Labels, and Both. You can specify the search method.

REVIEW

To replace data

(Part 1 of 2)

1. Move the cell pointer to the first cell in the range that you want to search.
2. Type **/RS** to select the Range Search command.
3. Point to the range or type the address of the range that you want to search.
4. Press **Enter**.
5. Type the desired search string and press **Enter**.

Replace data

(Part 2 of 2)

before

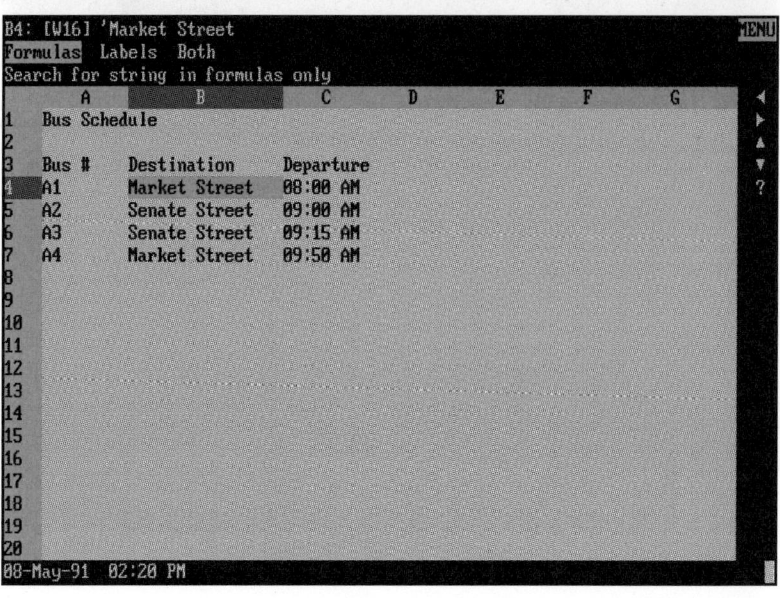

Oops!
To undo replacements, press the Alt-F4 key combination immediately after making the replacements.

Replacing data is a two-part process. The first part, Select the search range and string, is covered on the preceding two pages. These two pages cover the second part, Make replacements.

1. **Type L.**

   Typing L tells 1-2-3 to search only labels (or text) in the worksheet. You see these choices: Find and Replace.

2. **Type R.**

   Typing R selects Replace. You see the prompt `Enter replacement string:`.

3. **Type Baker Avenue.**

   Baker Avenue is the text that you want to use as the replacement.

4. **Press Enter.**

   Pressing Enter confirms the replacement string. 1-2-3 starts the search and stops on the first occurrence of the search string. You have these choices: Replace, All, Next, and Quit. The string is highlighted in the control panel.

5. **Type R.**

   Typing R replaces this text with the replacement text. 1-2-3 moves to the next occurrence. When the program finds the desired text, it stops and displays the choices.

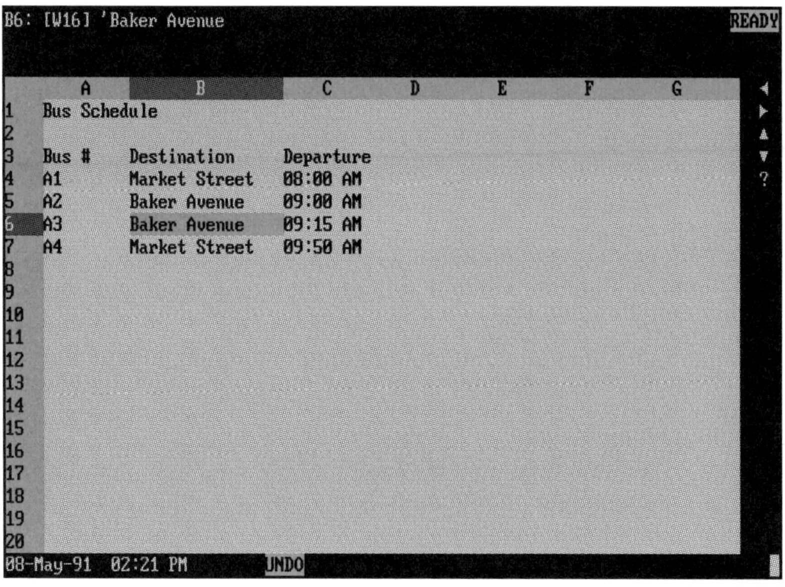

after

Save the worksheet
You should save the worksheet before you make any replacements. Then if you make a mistake, you can go back to the original version of the worksheet.

6. Type **R**.
   Typing R replaces this text with the replacement text. When 1-2-3 cannot find any more occurrences of the text, you see the message `No more matching strings.`
7. Press **Esc**.
   Pressing the Esc key clears the error message.

REVIEW

To replace data

(Part 2 of 2)

1. Type **F**, **L**, or **B** to search for Formulas, Labels, or Both.
2. Type **R** to select Replace.
3. Type the desired replacement string and press **Enter**.
4. When 1-2-3 finds the first occurrence of the text, type **R** to replace this occurrence, **A** to replace all occurrences, **N** to keep this text the same and move to the next occurrence, or **Q** to quit the search.
5. When the search ends, press **Esc** to clear the error message that is displayed.

Printing and Enhancing the Worksheet

This section covers the following tasks:

Attach Wysiwyg

Invoke Wysiwyg

Shade a cell

Underline cells

Outline cells

Change a font

Set margins

Insert a page break

Preview a worksheet

Print a worksheet

Attach Wysiwyg

before

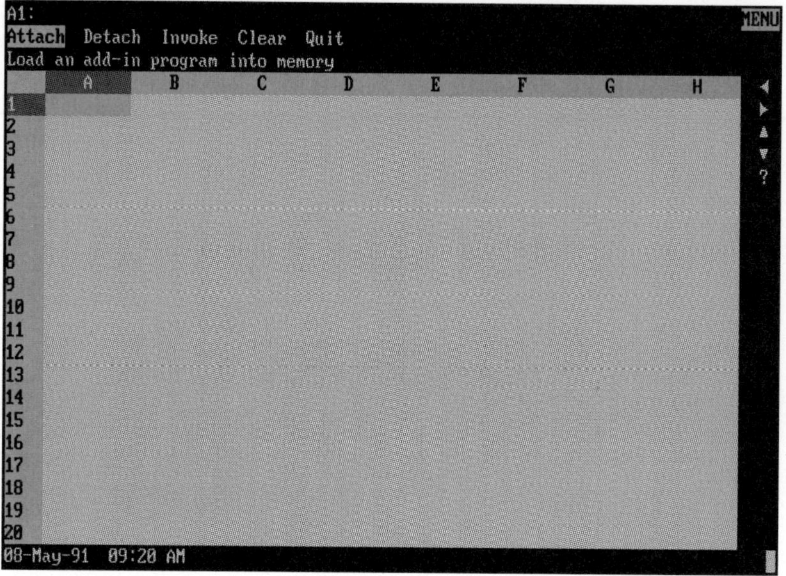

Oops!
To detach the add-in, type /AD to select Add-In Detach, type the add-in name, press Enter, and type Q.

1. **Type /A.**

   Typing /A selects the Add-In command. You see a list of menu options in the control panel.

2. **Type A.**

   Typing A selects Attach. This command tells 1-2-3 that you want to attach or load the add-in program. In the third line of the control panel, you see a list of available add-in programs.

3. **Type Wysiwyg.**

   Wysiwyg is the name of the program that you want to attach. You also can use the arrow keys to point to this add-in.

4. **Press Enter.**

   Pressing Enter confirms the add-in. You see these choices in the control panel: No-Key, 7, 8, 9, and 10. With these choices, you tell 1-2-3 how you will invoke the add-in.

5. **Type 7.**

   Typing 7 assigns the add-in to the function key combination Alt-F7. Pressing the Alt-F7 key combination will now invoke the add-in.

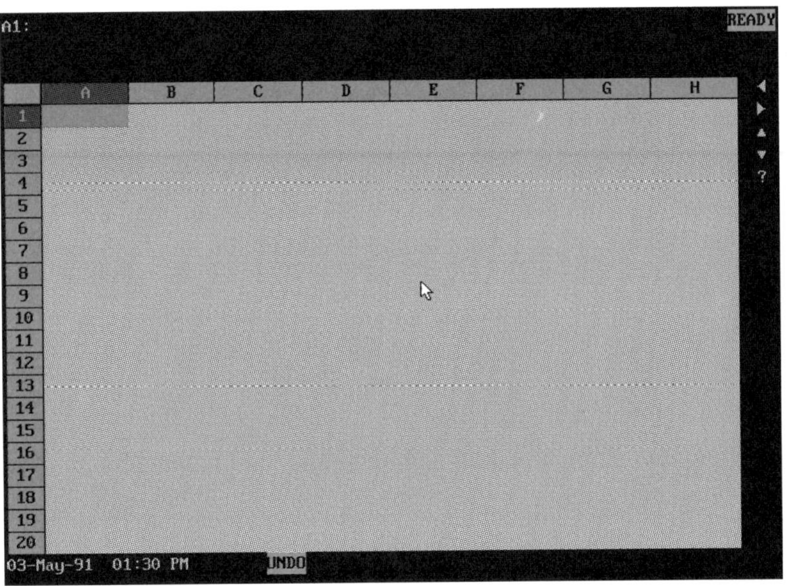

after

1-2-3 attaches (or loads) the program. The screen display changes to Wysiwyg mode. Wysiwyg stands for *What You See Is What You Get.* In this mode, you can see the worksheet as it will appear when printed.

6. Type **Q**.

   Typing Q closes the menu.

Who can use Wysiwyg? Wysiwyg is only available for 1-2-3 Version 2.3. If you are using an earlier version, you will not be able to use Wysiwyg features.

REVIEW

To attach Wysiwyg

1. Type **/AA** to select Add-In Attach.
2. Type **Wysiwyg** or point to the add-in name.
3. Press **Enter**.
4. Type **N** (No-Key), **7**, **8**, **9**, or **10** to select which function key to assign the add-in.
5. Type **Q** to close the menu.

What is an add-in? An add-in is a special utility program that works with the main program—in this case 1-2-3. The add-in program provides additional features.

TASK

Invoke Wysiwyg

before

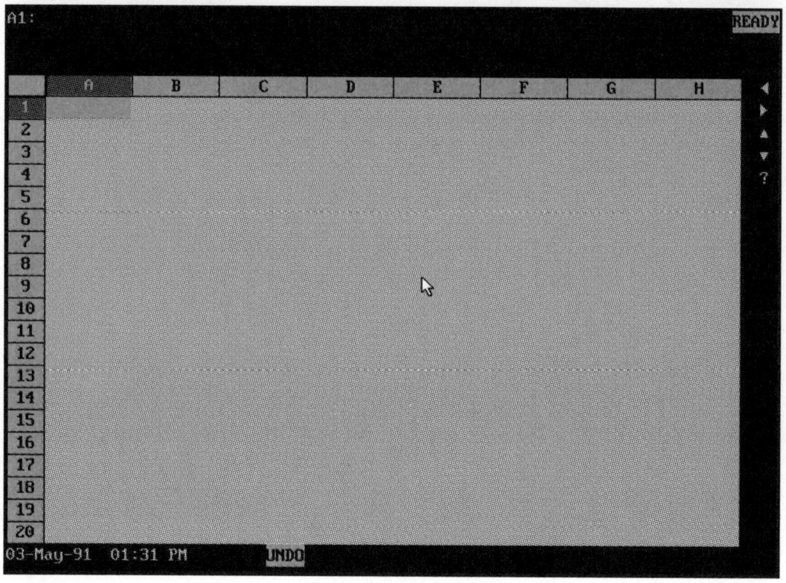

A1: READY

	A	B	C	D	E	F	G	H
1								
2								
3								
4								
5								
6								
7								
8								
9								
10								
11								
12								
13								
14								
15								
16								
17								
18								
19								
20								

03-May-91 01:31 PM UNDO

Oops!
To return to the 1-2-3 menu, press the Esc key and then press the / (forward slash) key.

1. **Attach Wysiwyg.**

   To invoke Wysiwyg, you first must attach this add-in option. See *TASK: Attach Wysiwyg* for more information. After it is attached, you see the screen in Wysiwig view.

2. **Type : (colon).**

   Typing a colon invokes Wysiwyg automatically. This procedure is the easiest method to invoke the add-in, and it requires the least number of keystrokes. The colon is similar to the slash key for 1-2-3. All Wysiwyg commands are preceded by a colon.

   When you press the colon key, the program starts. You see different commands in the control panel, and the menu pointer changes color on a color monitor. The mode indicator displays `WYSIWYG`.

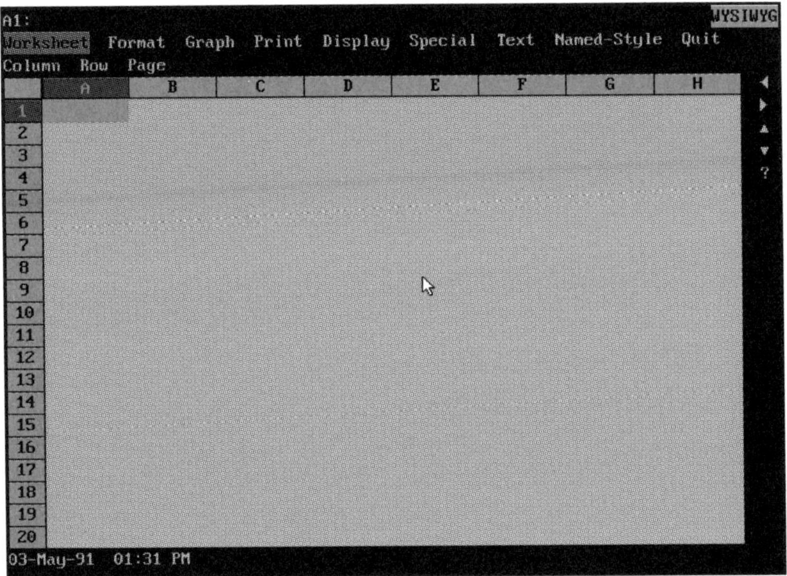

after

Who can use Wysiwyg? Wysiwyg is only available for 1-2-3 Version 2.3. If you are using an earlier version, you will not be able to use Wysiwyg features.

This book covers only a few of the enhancements that you can make with Wysiwyg. For complete information, see *Using 1-2-3 for DOS Release 2.3,* Special Edition.

You also can invoke Wysiwyg from the 1-2-3 menu system. To do so, type A to select the Add-In command. You see a list of options. Type I to select Invoke. Press Enter.

REVIEW

To invoke Wysiwyg

1. Attach Wysiwyg.
2. Type : (colon).

Attach vs. invoke Attaching an add-in program loads the program into memory. Invoking the add-in program activates or starts the program.

TASK

Shade a cell

before

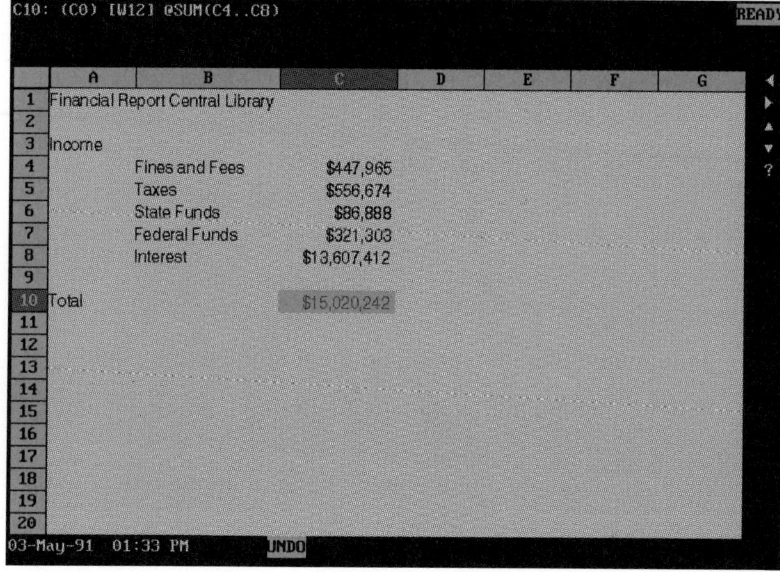

Oops!
To turn off the shade, press the Alt-F4 key combination.

1. **Attach Wysiwyg.**
   To shade a cell, you must use a special add-in program called Wysiwyg. For information on attaching this program, see *TASK: Attach Wysiwyg*.

2. **Use the arrow keys to move the cell pointer to cell C10.**
   C10 is the cell that you want to shade.

3. **Type : (colon).**
   Typing a colon invokes Wysiwyg. The Wysiwyg menu is activated automatically, and you see a list of different menu commands.

4. **Type FS.**
   Typing FS selects the Format Shade command. You see a list of shading options: Light, Dark, Solid, and Clear.

5. **Type L.**
   Typing L selects Light. You see the prompt `Change the attributes of range: C10..C10`. **C10** is the current cell.

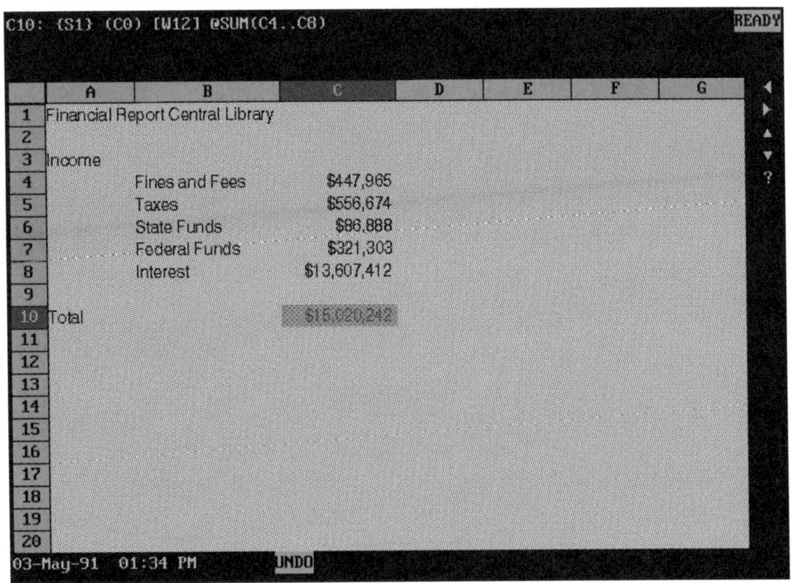

after

Who can use Wysiwyg? Wysiwyg is only available for 1-2-3 Version 2.3. If you are using an earlier version, you will not be able to use Wysiwyg features.

6. Press **Enter**.

   Pressing Enter selects the current cell C10. You can shade a range by selecting the range for this step and then pressing Enter.

   In Wysiwyg mode, you see the shading change on-screen. You see the notation {S1} within the control panel, which tells you that the change has occurred.

REVIEW

To shade a cell

1. Attach Wysiwyg.
2. Move the cell pointer to the first cell in the range that you want to change.
3. Type **:FS** to invoke Wysiwyg and select the Format Shade command.
4. Type **L**, **D**, **S**, or **C** to select Light, Dark, Solid, or Clear.
5. Point to the range or type the range address.
6. Press **Enter**.

Turn off the shade without Undo
You may have memory problems using both Undo and Wysiwyg. If you cannot use Undo, invoke Wysiwyg and type FSC to select Format Shade Clear. Type the range and press Enter.

Underline cells

before

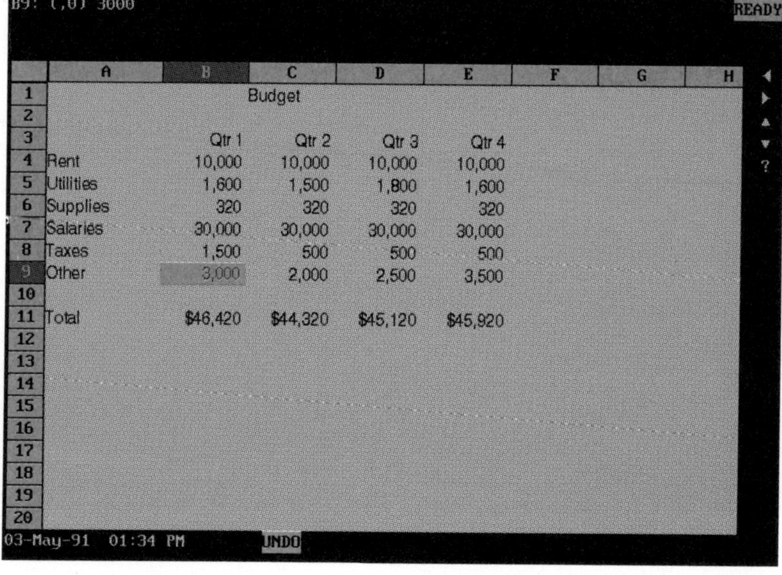

B9: (,0) 3000 READY

	A	B	C	D	E	F	G	H
1			Budget					
2								
3		Qtr 1	Qtr 2	Qtr 3	Qtr 4			
4	Rent	10,000	10,000	10,000	10,000			
5	Utilities	1,600	1,500	1,800	1,600			
6	Supplies	320	320	320	320			
7	Salaries	30,000	30,000	30,000	30,000			
8	Taxes	1,500	500	500	500			
9	Other	3,000	2,000	2,500	3,500			
10								
11	Total	$46,420	$44,320	$45,120	$45,920			
12								
13								
14								
15								
16								
17								
18								
19								
20								

03-May-91 01:34 PM UNDO

Oops!
To undo the line, press the Alt-F4 key combination.

1. **Attach Wysiwyg.**

   To use special format options, you must use a special add-in program called Wysiwyg. For information on attaching this program, see *TASK: Attach Wysiwyg*.

2. **Use the arrow keys to move the cell pointer to cell B9.**

   B9 is the first cell that you want to underline.

3. **Type : (colon).**

   Typing a colon invokes Wysiwyg. The Wysiwyg menu is activated automatically, and you see a list of different menu commands.

4. **Type FU.**

   Typing FU selects the Format Underline command.

   You see a list of line choices: Single, Double, Wide, and Clear.

5. **Type D.**

   Typing D selects Double from the list of choices. You see the prompt `Change the attributes of range: B9..B9`. B9 is the current cell.

6. **Press the → key three times.**

   Pressing the → key three times highlights the range B9..E9.

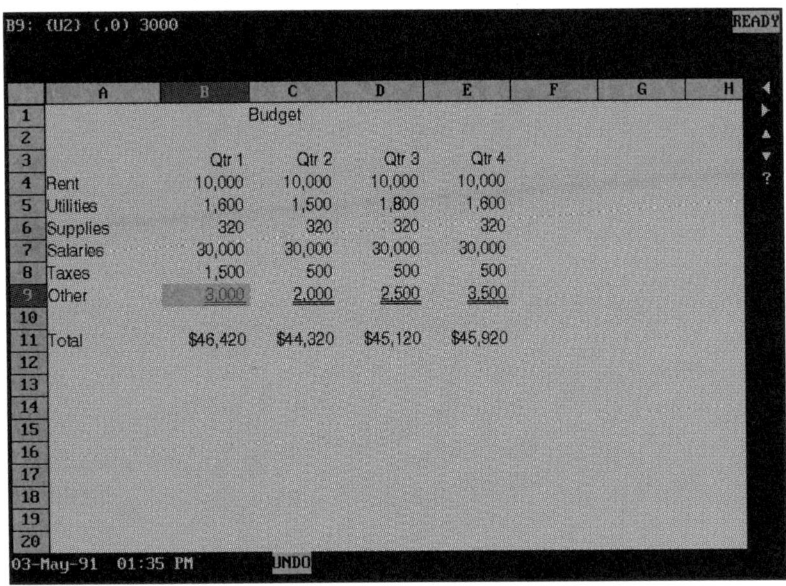

after

7. Press **Enter**.

   Pressing Enter confirms the selected range. 1-2-3 draws a double line under each cell. You see {U2} in the control panel, which indicates this format change.

Who can use Wysiwyg?
Wysiwyg is only available for 1-2-3 Version 2.3. If you are using an earlier version, you will not be able to use Wysiwyg features.

REVIEW

To underline cells

1. Attach Wysiwyg.
2. Move the cell pointer to the first cell in the range that you want to change.
3. Type **:FU** to invoke Wysiwyg and select the Format Underline command.
4. Select a line style. Type **S**, **D**, **W**, or **C** to select Single, Double, Wide, or Clear.
5. Point to the range or type the range address.
6. Press **Enter**.

Clear the line
You also can undo the underline by typing :FUC to select the Format Underline Clear command. Then type the range and press Enter.

TASK

Outline cells

before

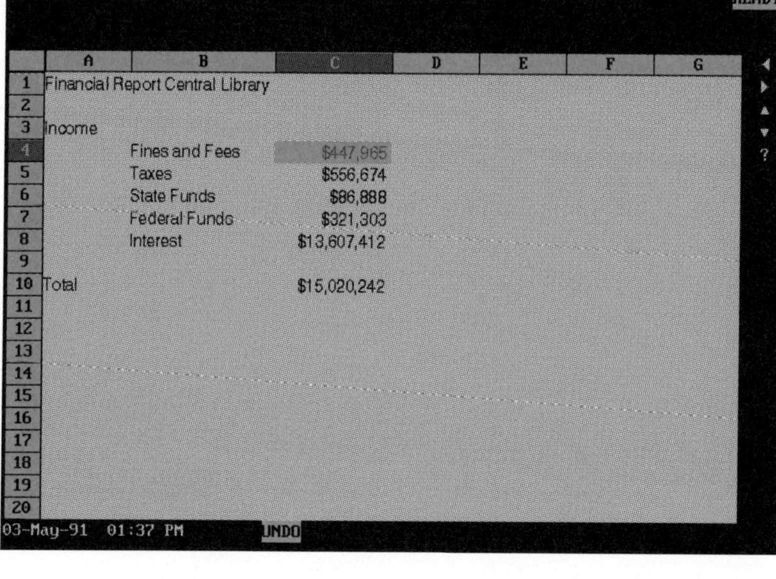

C4: (C0) [W12] 447965
READY
A B C D E F G
1 Financial Report Central Library
2
3 Income
4 Fines and Fees $447,965
5 Taxes $556,674
6 State Funds $86,888
7 Federal Funds $321,303
8 Interest $13,607,412
9
10 Total $15,020,242
11
12
13
14
15
16
17
18
19
20
03-May-91 01:37 PM
UNDO

Oops!
To undo the outline, press the Alt-F4 key combination immediately after applying formatting.

1. **Attach Wysiwyg.**
   To use special format options, you must use a special add-in program called Wysiwyg. For information on attaching this program, see *TASK: Attach Wysiwyg.*

2. **Use the arrow keys to move the cell pointer to cell C4.**
   C4 is the cell that you want to outline with a box.

3. **Type : (colon).**
   Typing a colon invokes Wysiwyg. The Wysiwyg menu is activated automatically, and you see a list of different menu commands.

4. **Type FL.**
   Typing FL selects the Format Lines command. You see a list of line options.

5. **Type O.**
   Typing O selects Outline. You see the prompt `Change the attributes of range: C4..C4`. C4 is the current cell.

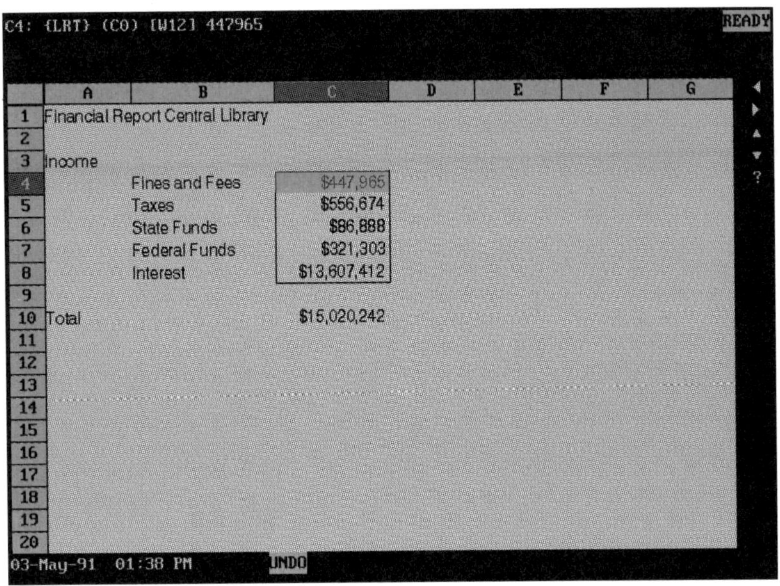

after

6. Press the ↓ key **four times**.

   Pressing the ↓ key four times selects the range C5..C8. This is the range that you will outline.

7. Press **Enter**.

   Pressing Enter tells 1-2-3 to outline the selected range. On-screen, the selected range is outlined. You see {LRT} in the control panel, which indicates this format change.

Who can use Wysiwyg?
Wysiwyg is only available for 1-2-3 Version 2.3. If you are using an earlier version, you will not be able to use Wysiwyg features.

REVIEW

To outline a cell

1. Attach Wysiwyg.
2. Type **:FLO** to invoke Wysiwyg and select the Format Lines Outline command.
3. Point to the range or type the range address.
4. Press **Enter**.

Clear the outline
You also can undo the outline by typing :FLC to select the Format Lines Clear command. Type O to select Outline; then type or point to the range and press Enter.

Change a font

Oops!
To change back to the original font, follow this same procedure and select the original font.

before

A1: 'Financial Report Central Library READY

	A	B	C	D	E	F	G
1	Financial Report Central Library						
2							
3	Income						
4		Fines and Fees	$447,965				
5		Taxes	$556,674				
6		State Funds	$86,888				
7		Federal Funds	$321,303				
8		Interest	$13,607,412				
9							
10	Total		$15,020,242				
11							
12							
13							
14							
15							
16							
17							
18							
19							
20							

03-May-91 01:38 PM UNDO

1. Attach Wysiwyg.

   To use special format options, you must use a special add-in program called Wysiwyg. For information on attaching this add-on, see *TASK: Attach Wysiwyg*.

2. Use the arrow keys to move the cell pointer to cell A1.

   A1 is the first cell in the range that you want to change. The default font is Bitstream Swiss 12 point.

3. Type : (colon).

   Typing a colon invokes Wysiwyg. The Wysiwyg menu is activated automatically, and you see a list of different menu commands.

4. Type **FF**.

   Typing FF selects the Format Font command. You see a list of available fonts on-screen. Your list may vary, depending on the fonts that you installed when you installed 1-2-3. For more information on installing fonts, see your 1-2-3 manual or *Using 1-2-3 for DOS Release 2.3,* Special Edition.

5. Type 3.

   Typing 3 selects Font 3, which is Bitstream Swiss 24 Point. (If you do not have this font, select one that does appear.) You see the prompt `Change the attributes of range: A1..A1`. **A1** is the current cell.

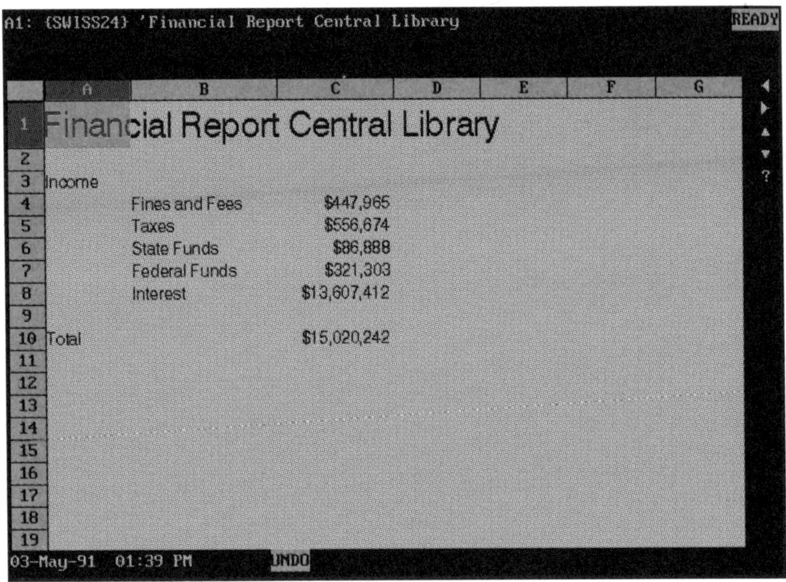

after

Who can use Wysiwyg? Wysiwyg is only available for 1-2-3 Version 2.3. If you are using an earlier version, you will not be able to use Wysiwyg features.

6. Press **Enter**.

   Pressing Enter confirms the font change. You see the font change on-screen. The formatted entry spills into the next cells. The control panel also indicates the change. You see `{Swiss24}` in the control panel. If you selected a different font in step 5, the display panel will display a different message.

REVIEW

To change a font

1. Attach Wysiwyg.
2. Move the cell pointer to the first cell in the range that you want to change.
3. Type **:FF** to invoke Wysiwyg and select the Format Font command.
4. Select a font.
5. Point to the range or type the range address.
6. Press **Enter**.

TASK

Set margins

before

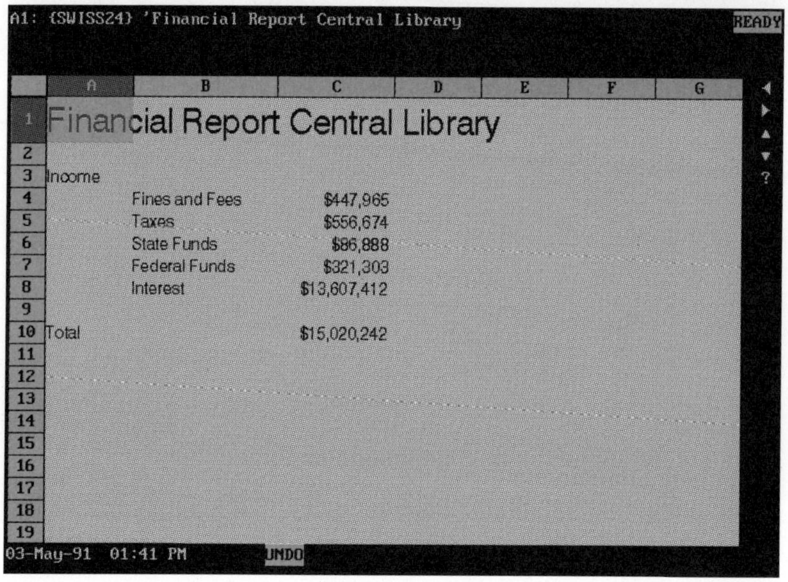

```
A1: {SWISS24} 'Financial Report Central Library                READY
     A        B            C          D      E      F      G
1   Financial Report Central Library
2
3   Income
4            Fines and Fees        $447,965
5            Taxes                 $556,674
6            State Funds            $86,888
7            Federal Funds         $321,303
8            Interest           $13,607,412
9
10  Total                       $15,020,242
11
12
13
14
15
16
17
18
19
03-May-91  01:41 PM          UNDO
```

Oops!
To change the margins, follow this same procedure and type the new margin setting.

1. Attach Wysiwyg.

   To use special format options, you must use a special add-in program called Wysiwyg. For information on attaching, see *TASK: Attach Wysiwyg*.

   You also can change the margins through the 1-2-3 Print menu. For most enhancements, it is better to use Wysiwyg because this add-in provides quality output, such as better-looking fonts. Wysiwyg also lets you set your margins in inches rather than characters. This method is a more precise way to set measurements.

   See *Using 1-2-3 for DOS Release 2.3,* Special Edition, for information about changing margins through the Print menu.

2. Type : (colon).

   Typing a colon invokes Wysiwyg. The Wysiwyg menu is activated automatically, and you see a list of different menu commands.

3. Type **PL**.

   Typing PL selects the Print Layout command. On-screen you see the Wysiwyg Print Settings dialog box.

4. Type **M**.

   Typing M selects Margins. You see these choices in the control panel: Left, Right, Top, Bottom, and Quit.

5. Type **T**.

   Typing T selects the Top margin. This is the margin that you want to change. You are prompted `Enter top margin: 0.5`. The default is one-half inch (.5).

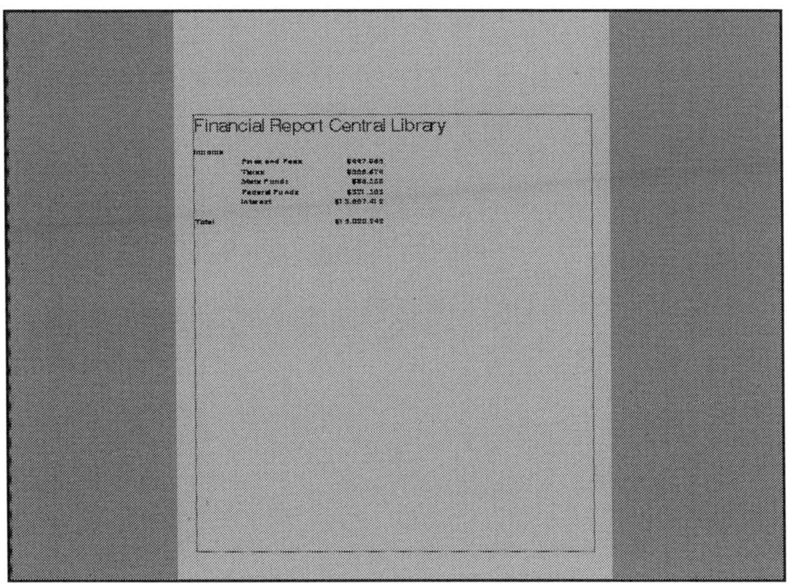

after

6. Type **2**.
   Typing 2 sets the new margin to two inches.

7. Press **Enter**.
   Pressing Enter confirms the new margin. The new margin appears in the dialog box.

8. Type **Q three times**.
   Typing Q three times closes all the menus. You cannot see the margin change on-screen.

Who can use Wysiwyg?
Wysiwyg is only available for 1-2-3 Version 2.3. If you are using an earlier version, you will not be able to use Wysiwyg features.

REVIEW

To set margins

1. Attach Wysiwyg.
2. Type **:PLM**.
3. Select any of the margin options and type a new value.

Margin	*Default*
Left	.5
Right	.5
Top	.5
Bottom	.55

4. Press **Enter**.
5. Type **Q three times** to exit all menus.

Preview the worksheet
To see the margin changes on-screen, you need to preview the worksheet. See *TASK: Preview a worksheet.*

Insert a page break

before

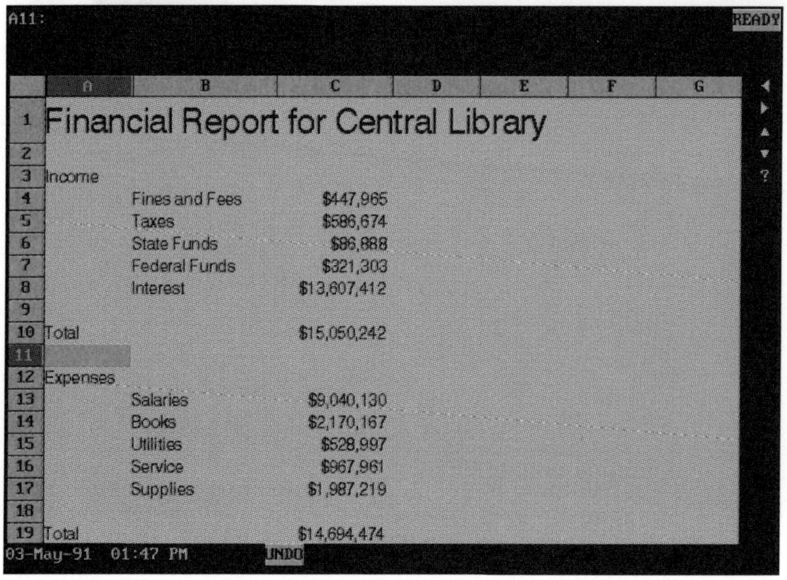

A11: READY

	A	B	C	D	E	F	G
1	Financial Report for Central Library						
2							
3	Income						
4		Fines and Fees	$447,965				
5		Taxes	$586,674				
6		State Funds	$86,888				
7		Federal Funds	$321,303				
8		Interest	$13,607,412				
9							
10	Total		$15,050,242				
11							
12	Expenses						
13		Salaries	$9,040,130				
14		Books	$2,170,167				
15		Utilities	$528,997				
16		Service	$967,961				
17		Supplies	$1,987,219				
18							
19	Total		$14,694,474				

03-May-91 01:47 PM UNDO

Oops!
To delete the page break, type :WPD to select the Worksheet Page Delete command.

1. Attach Wysiwyg.

   To use special format options, you must use a special add-in program called Wysiwyg. For information on attaching, see *TASK: Attach Wysiwyg.*

   You can set page breaks using the Worksheet Page command. For most enhancements, it is better to use Wysiwyg because this add-in provides quality output, such as better-looking fonts. Also, with Wysiwyg the page break appears on-screen as a dashed line, which lets you see the page break.

   See *Using 1-2-3 for DOS Release 2.3,* Special Edition, for information about changing margins through the Print menu.

2. Use the arrow keys to move the cell pointer to A11.

   Cell A11 is the cell where you want to insert a page break. Everything above cell A11 prints on one page; everything below it prints on another page.

3. Type : (colon).

   Typing a colon invokes Wysiwyg. The Wysiwyg menu is activated automatically, and you see a list of different menu commands.

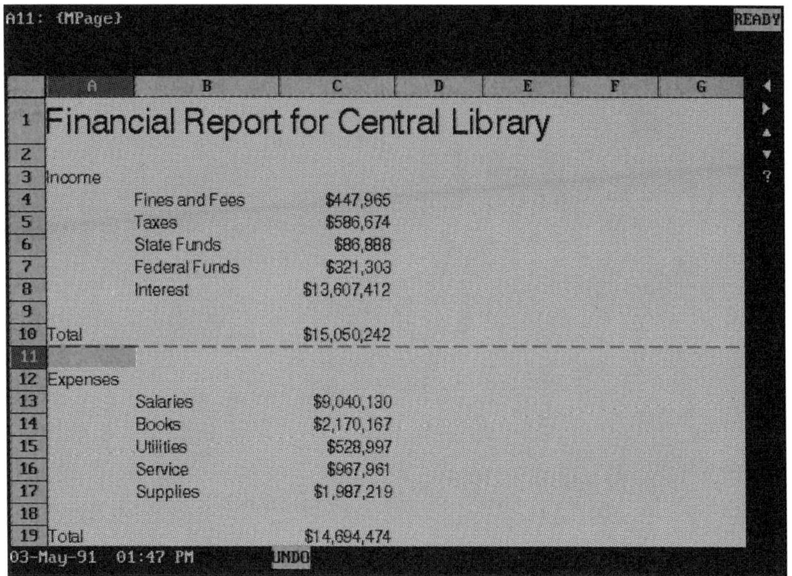

after

Who can use Wysiwyg? Wysiwyg is only available for 1-2-3 Version 2.3. If you are using an earlier version, you will not be able to use Wysiwyg features.

4. Type **WPR**.

   Typing WPR selects the Worksheet Page Row command. On-screen, you see a dashed line above the row. This line shows where the page break occurs. You see the code {MPAGE} in the control panel.

5. Type **Q**.

   Typing Q selects Quit and returns you to the worksheet.

REVIEW

To insert a page break

1. Attach Wysiwyg.
2. Move the cell pointer to the row where you want to insert the page break.
3. Type **:WP** to invoke Wysiwyg and select the Worksheet Page command.
4. Type R to break the page at the current row or C to break at the current column.
5. Type **Q** to return to the worksheet.

TASK

Preview a worksheet

before

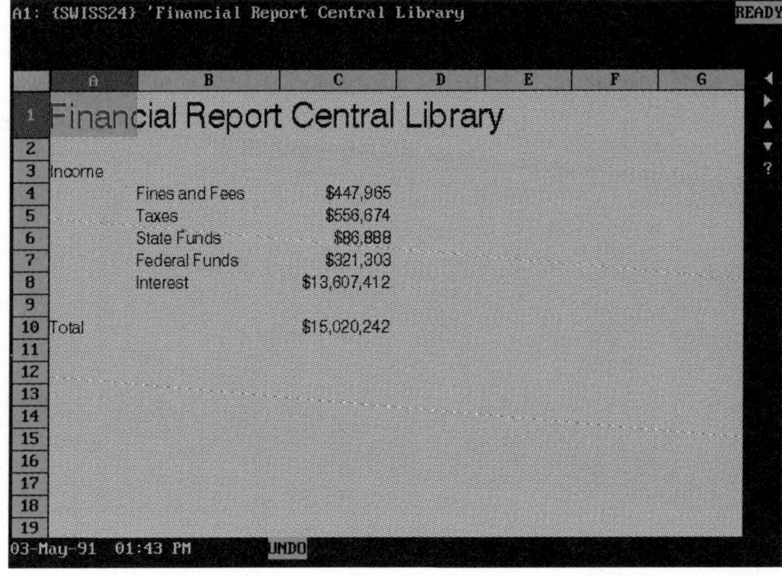

Oops!
To quit the preview, press the Esc key.

1. **Attach Wysiwyg.**

   To preview a worksheet, you must use a special add-in program called Wysiwyg. For information on attaching this program, see *TASK: Attach Wysiwyg*.

2. **Type : (colon).**

   Typing a colon invokes Wysiwyg. The Wysiwyg menu is activated automatically, and you see a list of different menu commands.

3. **Type P.**

   Typing P selects the Print command. You see a list of print options in the control panel. The Wysiwyg Print Settings dialog box appears in the middle of the screen.

4. **Type R.**

   Typing R selects Range. You see these choices: Set and Clear.

5. **Type S.**

   Typing S selects Set. You see the prompt `Specify the range to print: A1`. 1-2-3 is now in `POINT` mode.

6. **Type A1..E10.**

   A1..E10 is the range that you want to print. You also can point to the range by using the mouse or the arrow keys.

7. **Press Enter.**

   Pressing Enter confirms the range. The range is listed in the dialog box in the Print Range box.

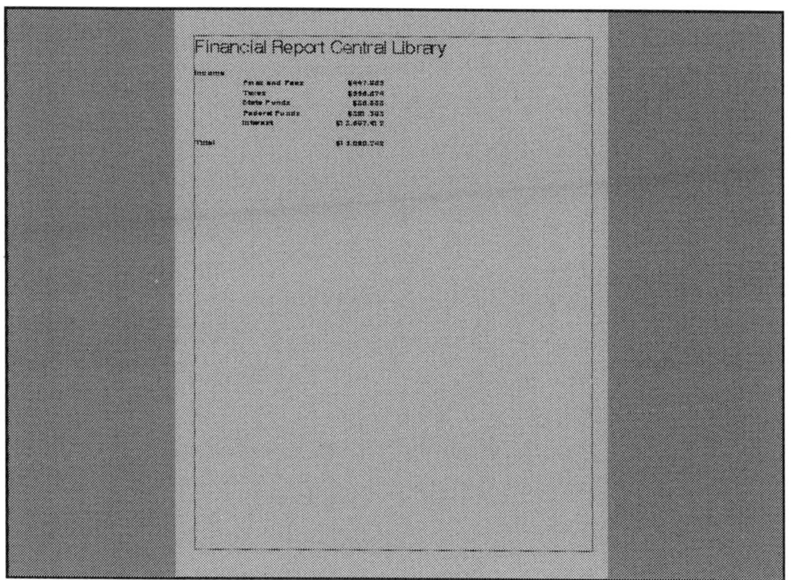

after

Who can use Wysiwyg?
Wysiwyg is only available for 1-2-3 Version 2.3. If you are using an earlier version, you will not be able to use Wysiwyg features.

8. Type **P**.

   Typing P selects Preview. This selection tells 1-2-3 to display the worksheet on-screen. You see a graphic representation of the worksheet. Items such as font changes, headers, and footers are displayed in this view.

   To display this view, your monitor must have graphics capability. If you get an error message or nothing appears, your monitor may not be able to display graphics. In this case, you have to print your worksheet to see formatting changes.

Specify a range
If the worksheet does not display, you may not have specified a range. You must specify the range to print (display).

9. Press **Esc three times**.

   Pressing the Esc key three times closes this view and returns you to the worksheet. A dashed line appears around specified print ranges; in this case, it appears around A1..E10.

REVIEW

To preview a worksheet

1. Attach Wysiwyg.
2. Type **:PRS**.
3. Type or point to the range and press **Enter**.
4. Type **P** to select the Preview command.
5. Press the **Esc** key to quit the preview.
6. Type **Q** to close the menu.

TASK

Print a worksheet

before

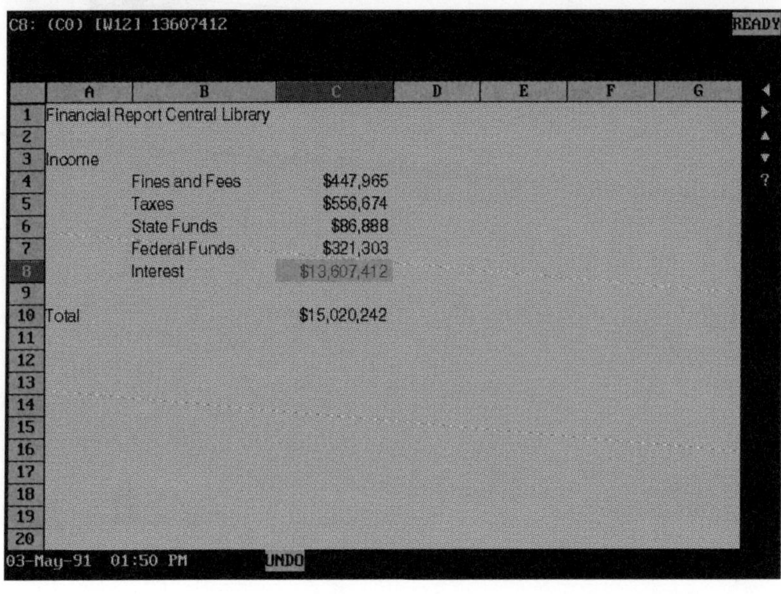

Oops!
To stop a print job, press Ctrl-Break. Then press the Esc key to clear the error message that appears.

1. Make sure that you have installed a graphics printer.
   For complete installation instructions, see your 1-2-3 manual.
2. Attach Wysiwyg.
   For better-looking output, use Wysiwyg. This add-in provides quality output, such as better-looking fonts.
3. Type : (colon).
   Typing a colon invokes Wysiwyg. The Wysiwyg menu is activated automatically, and you see a list of different menu commands.
4. Type **P**.
   Typing P opens the Print menu.
5. Type **RS**.
   Typing RS selects Range Set.
6. Type **A1..E10**.
   A1..E10 is the range that you want to print.
7. Press **Enter**.
   Pressing Enter confirms the range.
8. Type **CP**.
   Typing CP selects the Config Printer command. You see a list of installed printers on-screen.

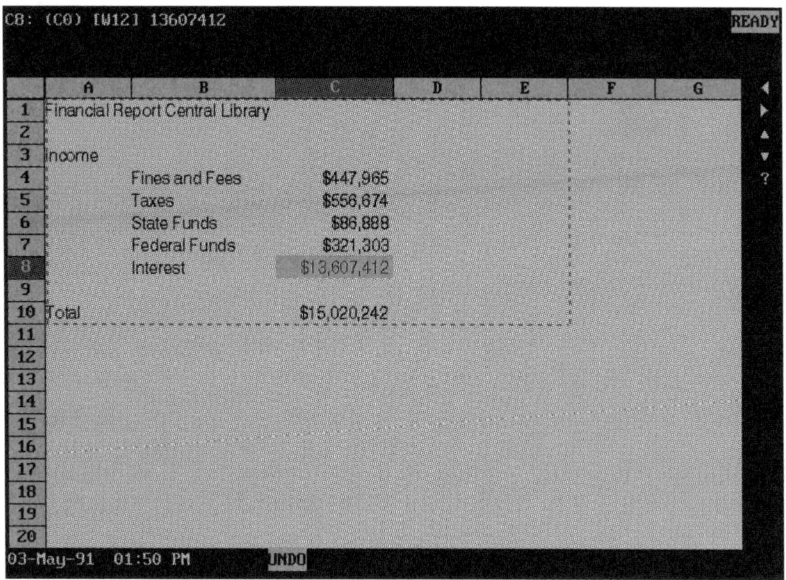

after

9. Use the arrow keys to select the printer you use.
   For more information on installing a printer, see your 1-2-3 manual.

10. Press **Enter**.
    Pressing Enter confirms your printer selection.

11. Press **Esc**.
    Pressing the Esc key redisplays the Print menu commands.

12. Type **G**.
    Typing G selects Go. The worksheet is printed.

Who can use Wysiwyg?
Wysiwyg is only available for 1-2-3 Version 2.3. If you are using an earlier version, you will not be able to use Wysiwyg features.

REVIEW

To print a worksheet

1. Install a graphics printer.
2. Attach Wysiwyg.
3. Type **:PRS**.
4. Type or point and press **Enter**.
5. Type **CP** to select the Config Printer command.
6. Select your printer and press **Enter**.
7. Press **Q** to return to the Print menu.
8. Type **G** to print the worksheet.

Specify a range
If you get the error message saying that no print range was selected, you did not specify a range to print. Press the Esc key and start over.

Reference

Quick Reference

Glossary

Quick Reference

If you cannot remember how to access a particular feature, use this reference list to find the appropriate keystrokes. For more detailed information, see the Task/Review part of this book.

Task	*Keystrokes*
Center	/RLC
Column Delete	/WDC
Column Hide	/WCH
Column Insert	/WIC
Column Width	/WCS
Comma Format	/RF, (comma)
Copy	/C
Currency Format	/RFC
Data Fill	/DF
Data Sort	/DS
Date Format	/RFD
Edit	F2 key
Exit	/Q
File Retrieve	/FR
GoTo	F5 key
Help	F1 key
Move	/M
Page break	/WP
Percent Format	/RFP
Print	/P
Range Erase	/RE
Range Protect	/RP
Right Align	/RLR
Row Delete	/WDR
Row Insert	/WIR
Save	/FS
Search and Replace	/RS
Time Format	/RFDT
Undo	Alt-F4 key combination
Worksheet Erase	/WE

Glossary

add-in A special utility program that works with the main program. In this case, the main program is 1-2-3. The add-in program provides features that aren't available in the main program.

cell The intersection of any column and row. Each cell in a worksheet has a unique address. A cell address is formed by combining the column and row locations into one description. For example, A8 describes the intersection of column A and row 8.

cell pointer A highlighted rectangle that indicates the active cell. The cell pointer shows where you can enter data or where a range begins.

control panel The top three lines of the 1-2-3 screen. These lines display menu choices. They also display information about the current cell, such as the cell's address, the current entry, and the current formatting (numeric format, column width, and so on).

copy An operation that duplicates a cell or a range. The entry appears in both the original location and the new location.

default The initial settings that are in effect when you install 1-2-3.

directory A disk area that stores files. A directory is like a drawer in a file cabinet. Within that drawer, you can store several files.

DOS An acronym for Disk Operating System. DOS manages the details of your system, such as storing and retrieving programs and files.

file The various individual reports, worksheets, databases, and documents that you store on your hard drive or floppy disk for future use.

file name The name that you assign a file when you store it to disk. A file name consists of two parts: the root name and the extension. The root name can be up to eight characters in length. The extension can be up to three characters in length and usually indicates the file type. The root name and extension are separated by a period. SALES.WK1 is a valid file name. SALES is the root name, and WK1 is the extension.

font The size and typeface of a set of characters.

footer Text that appears at the bottom of every page.

formula An entry that performs a calculation on two or more values or series of values. A formula can reference cells or values.

function A built-in formula that is included with 1-2-3. Functions perform specialized calculations for you, such as loan payments.

graph A visual representation of your data. You can display selected data using one of many graph types, such as a bar graph, pie graph, line graph, and so on.

header Text that appears at the top of every page.

label A text entry.

menu An on-screen list of 1-2-3 options. Menus appear horizontally in the control panel.

mode indicator A code that appears in the control panel and indicates which program mode 1-2-3 is in. READY, for example, indicates that the worksheet is ready for input.

mouse An input device, that enables you to move the cell pointer on-screen, select menu commands, and perform other operations.

move An operation that moves a cell or a range from one location to another. The cell range is deleted from the old location and appears only in the new location.

numeric format The way that values are displayed. You can select to display dollar signs, decimal points, commas, percentages, and so on.

path The route, through directories, to a program or document file. For example, the path C:\123R23\DATA\REPORT.WK1 includes four elements: the disk drive (C:); the first directory (123R23); the subdirectory, which is a directory within the first directory (DATA); and the file name (REPORT.WK1).

prompt An on-screen message that gives you information about the program's status or reminds you to perform an action.

range Any rectangular area of columns and rows. A range can be a cell, a row, a column, or a combination of contiguous columns and rows. After you select a range, you can perform different actions, such as copy it, erase it, enhance it, and so on. The Task/Review part of this book covers range operations.

range address The method that 1-2-3 uses to identify a range. The first element in the range address is the location of the uppermost left cell in the range; the second element is the location of the lowermost right cell. For example, the range A1..C3 includes the cells A1, A2, A3, B1, B2, B3, C1, C2, and C3.

replacement string A set of characters that replaces the search string when you perform a search and replace.

search string A set of characters, such as a word or value, for which 1-2-3 looks in search and replace operations.

settings sheet An on-screen list that displays the current status of 1-2-3 settings.

spreadsheet program An electronic version of an accountant's ledger. A spreadsheet program enables you to enter and manipulate data. You can perform tasks such as calculate, sort, and so on.

status indicator A code that appears in the status line and tells you the current status of the program features. For example, the status indicator NUM tells you that you pressed the Num Lock key and turned on the number lock function.

Undo A 1-2-3 feature that enables you to reverse the last worksheet entry.

value A number, formula, or date and time entry.

worksheet The blank screen of columns and rows that appears when you first start 1-2-3. A worksheet is also all the data and formatting information that you enter on-screen. 1-2-3 and your operating system keep track of worksheets by storing them on disk in files.

Wysiwyg An add-in program that enables you to enhance your worksheet by changing fonts, adding headers, shading cells, and so on. Wysiwyg stands for "What You See Is What You Get."

Index

Symbols

A

B

C

G

H

I

J-K

L

M

N

O

P

Q-R

S

T

U

V

W

Computer Books From Que Mean PC Performance!

Spreadsheets

1-2-3 Database Techniques	$29.95
1-2-3 Graphics Techniques	$24.95
1-2-3 Macro Library, 3rd Edition	$39.95
1-2-3 Release 2.2 Business Applications	$39.95
1-2-3 Release 2.2 PC Tutor	$39.95
1-2-3 Release 2.2 QueCards	$19.95
1-2-3 Release 2.2 Quick Reference	$ 8.95
1-2-3 Release 2.2 QuickStart, 2nd Edition	$19.95
1-2-3 Release 2.2 Workbook and Disk	$29.95
1-2-3 Release 3 Business Applications	$39.95
1-2-3 Release 3 Workbook and Disk	$29.95
1-2-3 Release 3.1 Quick Reference	$ 8.95
1-2-3 Release 3.1 QuickStart, 2nd Edition	$19.95
1-2-3 Tips, Tricks, and Traps, 3rd Edition	$24.95
Excel Business Applications: IBM Version	$39.95
Excel Quick Reference	$ 8.95
Excel QuickStart	$19.95
Excel Tips, Tricks, and Traps	$22.95
Using 1-2-3/G	$29.95
Using 1-2-3, Special Edition	$27.95
Using 1-2-3 Release 2.2, Special Edition	$27.95
Using 1-2-3 Release 3.1, 2nd Edition	$29.95
Using Excel: IBM Version	$29.95
Using Lotus Spreadsheet for DeskMate	$22.95
Using Quattro Pro	$24.95
Using SuperCalc5, 2nd Edition	$29.95

Databases

dBASE III Plus Handbook, 2nd Edition	$24.95
dBASE III Plus Tips, Tricks, and Traps	$24.95
dBASE III Plus Workbook and Disk	$29.95
dBASE IV Applications Library, 2nd Edition	$39.95
dBASE IV Programming Techniques	$24.95
dBASE IV Quick Reference	$ 8.95
dBASE IV QuickStart	$19.95
dBASE IV Tips, Tricks,and Traps, 2nd Edition.	$24.95
dBASE IV Workbook and Disk	$29.95
Using Clipper	$24.95
Using DataEase	$24.95
Using dBASE IV	$27.95
Using Paradox 3	$24.95
Using R:BASE	$29.95
Using Reflex, 2nd Edition	$24.95
Using SQL	$29.95

Business Applications

Allways Quick Reference	$ 8.95
Introduction to Business Software	$14.95
Introduction to Personal Computers	$19.95
Lotus Add-in Toolkit Guide	$29.95
Norton Utilities Quick Reference	$ 8.95
PC Tools Quick Reference, 2nd Edition	$ 8.95
Q&A Quick Reference	$ 8.95
Que's Computer User's Dictionary	$ 9.95
Que's Wizard Book	$ 9.95
Quicken Quick Reference	$ 8.95
SmartWare Tips, Tricks, and Traps 2nd Edition	$24.95
Using Computers in Business	$22.95
Using DacEasy, 2nd Edition	$24.95
Using Enable/OA	$29.95
Using Harvard Project Manager	$24.95
Using Managing Your Money, 2nd Edition	$19.95
Using Microsoft Works: IBM Version	$22.95
Using Norton Utilities	$24.95
Using PC Tools Deluxe	$24.95
Using Peachtree	$27.95
Using PFS: First Choice	$22.95
Using PROCOMM PLUS	$19.95
Using Q&A, 2nd Edition	$23.95
Using Quicken: IBM Version, 2nd Edition	$19.95
Using Smart	$22.95
Using SmartWare II	$29.95
Using Symphony, Special Edition	$29.95
Using Time Line	$24.95
Using TimeSlips	$24.95

CAD

AutoCAD Quick Reference	$ 8.95
AutoCAD Sourcebook 1991	$27.95
Using AutoCAD, 3rd Edition	$29.95
Using Generic CADD	$24.95

Word Processing

Microsoft Word 5 Quick Reference	$ 8.95
Using DisplayWrite 4, 2nd Edition	$24.95
Using LetterPerfect	$22.95
Using Microsoft Word 5.5: IBM Version, 2nd Edition	$24.95
Using MultiMate	$24.95
Using Professional Write	$22.95
Using Word for Windows	$24.95
Using WordPerfect 5	$27.95
Using WordPerfect 5.1, Special Edition	$27.95
Using WordStar, 3rd Edition	$27.95
WordPerfect PC Tutor	$39.95
WordPerfect Power Pack	$39.95
WordPerfect Quick Reference	$ 8.95
WordPerfect QuickStart	$19.95
WordPerfect 5 Workbook and Disk	$29.95
WordPerfect 5.1 Quick Reference	$ 8.95
WordPerfect 5.1 QuickStart	$19.95
WordPerfect 5.1 Tips, Tricks, and Traps	$24.95
WordPerfect 5.1 Workbook and Disk	$29.95

Hardware/Systems

DOS Tips, Tricks, and Traps	$24.95
DOS Workbook and Disk, 2nd Edition	$29.95
Fastback Quick Reference	$ 8.95
Hard Disk Quick Reference	$ 8.95
MS-DOS PC Tutor	$39.95
MS-DOS Power Pack	$39.95
MS-DOS Quick Reference	$ 8.95
MS-DOS QuickStart, 2nd Edition	$19.95
MS-DOS User's Guide, Special Edition	$29.95
Networking Personal Computers, 3rd Edition	$24.95
The Printer Bible	$29.95
Que's PC Buyer's Guide	$12.95
Understanding UNIX: A Conceptual Guide, 2nd Edition	$21.95
Upgrading and Repairing PCs	$29.95
Using DOS	$22.95
Using Microsoft Windows 3, 2nd Edition	$24.95
Using Novell NetWare	$29.95
Using OS/2	$29.95
Using PC DOS, 3rd Edition	$24.95
Using Prodigy	$19.95
Using UNIX	$29.95
Using Your Hard Disk	$29.95
Windows 3 Quick Reference	$ 8.95

Desktop Publishing/Graphics

CorelDRAW Quick Reference	$ 8.95
Harvard Graphics Quick Reference	$ 8.95
Using Animator	$24.95
Using DrawPerfect	$24.95
Using Harvard Graphics, 2nd Edition	$24.95
Using Freelance Plus	$24.95
Using PageMaker: IBM Version, 2nd Edition	$24.95
Using PFS: First Publisher, 2nd Edition	$24.95
Using Ventura Publisher, 2nd Edition	$24.95

Macintosh/Apple II

AppleWorks QuickStart	$19.95
The Big Mac Book, 2nd Edition	$29.95
Excel QuickStart	$19.95
The Little Mac Book	$ 9.95
Que's Macintosh Multimedia Handbook	$24.95
Using AppleWorks, 3rd Edition	$24.95
Using Excel: Macintosh Version	$24.95
Using FileMaker	$24.95
Using MacDraw	$24.95
Using MacroMind Director	$29.95
Using MacWrite	$24.95
Using Microsoft Word 4: Macintosh Version	$24.95
Using Microsoft Works: Macintosh Version, 2nd Edition	$24.95
Using PageMaker: Macinsoth Version, 2nd Edition	$24.95

Programming/Technical

Assembly Language Quick Reference	$ 8.95
C Programmer' sToolkit	$39.95
C Quick Reference	$ 8.95
DOS and BIOS Functions Quick Reference	$ 8.95
DOS Programmer's Reference, 2nd Edition	$29.95
Network Programming in C	$49.95
Oracle Programmer's Guide	$29.95
QuickBASIC Advanced Techniques	$24.95
Quick C Programmer's Guide	$29.95
Turbo Pascal Advanced Techniques	$24.95
Turbo Pascal Quick Reference	$ 8.95
UNIX Programmer's Quick Reference	$ 8.95
UNIX Programmer's Reference	$29.95
UNIX Shell Commands Quick Reference	$ 8.95
Using Assembly Language, 2nd Edition	$29.95
Using BASIC	$24.95
Using C	$29.95
Using QuickBASIC 4	$24.95
Using Turbo Pascal	$29.95

For More Information,
Call Toll Free!

1-800-428-5331

All prices and titles subject to change without notice. Non-U.S. prices may be higher. Printed in the U.S.A.

Que—The Top Name In Spreadsheet Information!

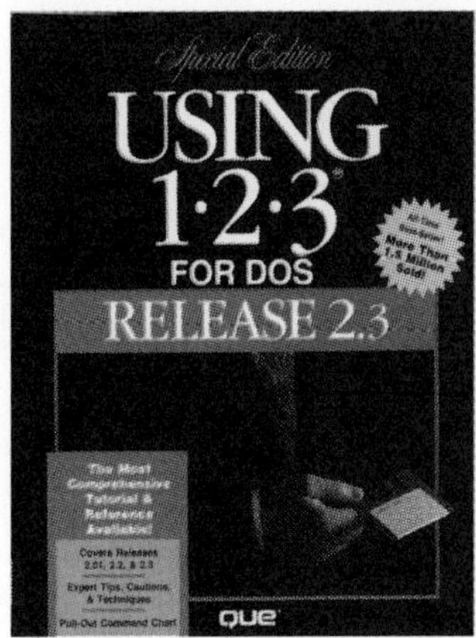

Using 1-2-3 for DOS Release 2.3, Special Edition

Que Development Group

This all-time best-seller offers the most comprehensive combination of tutorial and reference for 1-2-3 worksheet design and operations. It includes a **Troubleshooting** section and a complete **Command Reference**.

Through Release 2.3

Order #1354 **$29.95 USA**

0-88022-727-3, 900 pp., 7 3/8 x 9 1/4

1-2-3 Release 2.2 Quick Start, 2nd Edition

Que Development Group

Packed with illustrative examples and exercises, this text teachcs readers how to develop and use 1-2-3. The book is organized in modular sections that focus on the fundamentals of 1-2-3.

Releases 2.01 & 2.2

Order #1207 **$19.95 USA**

0-88022-612-9, 400 pp., 7 3/8 x 9 1/4

Book & Disk

1-2-3 Release 2.2 PC Tutor

Que Development Group

This quick-learning guide to 1-2-3 spreadsheets comes complete with tutorial disk, book lessons, and hands-on exercises for creating worksheets, graphs, databases, and printing reports.

Releases 2.01 & 2.2

Order #1232 **$39.95 USA**

0-88022-625-0, 300 pp., 7 3/8 x 9 1/4

1-2-3 Release 2.2 QueCards

Que Development Group

Releases 2.01 & 2.2

Order #1211 **$19.95 USA**

0-88022-616-1, 60 cards, 6 1/2 x 9

1-2-3 Release 2.2 Quick Reference

Que Development Group

Releases 2.01 & 2.2

Order #1042 **$8.95 USA**

0-88022-503-3, 160 pp., 4 3/4 x 8

1-2-3 for DOS Release 2.3 Quick Reference

Que Development Group

Through Release 2.3

Order #1352 **$9.95 USA**

0-88022-725-7, 160 pp., 4 3/4 x 8

Using 1-2-3 Release 2.2, Special Edition

Que Development Group

Releases 2.01 & 2.2

Order #1040 **$27.95 USA**

0-88022-501-7, 1,096 pp., 7 3/8 x 9 1/4

To Order, Call:
(800) 428-5331 OR (317) 573-2510

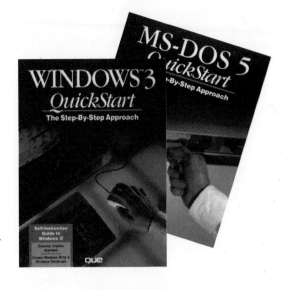